How You Can Invest
In Inflation-Proof
Vacations for Life

RESORT
TIMESHARING

by Keith W.
Trowbridge, Ph.D.

SIMON AND SCHUSTER | New York

Published by Simon and Schuster
A Division of Gulf & Western Corporation
Simon & Schuster Building
Rockefeller Center
1230 Avenue of the Americas
New York, New York 10020

SIMON AND SCHUSTER and colophon are trademarks of
Simon & Schuster
Designed by Irving Perkins Associates
Manufactured in the United States of America

1   2   3   4   5   6   7   8   9   10

Library of Congress Cataloging in Publication Data
Trowbridge, Keith W.
Resort timesharing.

Bibliography: p.
1. Timesharing (Real estate)—United States.
2. Second homes—United States.   Title.
HD7287.67.U5T76   333.3′234   81-16661
AACR2
ISBN 0-671 -43984-7

Contents

5. Worldwide Exchange Networks: The Icing on the Cake?   113

6. Buying in a Foreign Country   135

7. Should You Buy from a Local Broker?   141

8. How to Plan for Resales and Rentals   145

9. Your Legal Guidelines and Protection   153

10. **What Is the Future of Timesharing?**   169

11. **Who Are the People Involved?**   177

Foreword

Someone once quipped that "the only sure things in life are death and taxes." In this century, you could add "inflation" to that aphorism.

Modern technology hasn't provided eternal life, but it has extended the average life span considerably; taxes may not be avoidable, but knowledgeable people find some relief through special investments. However, the average family can only keep up with inflation through increased wages or by more careful planning of its budget.

This book is written to explain what is perhaps the most innovative approach to beating the vacation-inflation syndrome—interval resort timesharing. The average family now places more importance on its vacations than ever before—from improving the quality to increasing the frequency. Increasingly, the move toward more vacation time has been built into the breadwinner's job; everyone from the government worker to the union member to the self-employed and the corporate management employee has more vacation time.

The only bugaboo thwarting the enjoyment of better or more frequent vacations is *cost*. The average family is still behind the 8-ball in terms of discretionary dollars—those left over from each paycheck after the essential bills are paid. Inflation has increased the cost of all the elements of vacations: transportation, recreation, food and especially the price of decent accommodations.

As a developer and marketer of interval timeshare resorts, I may be expected to hold a certain bias, that of showing only the brighter side of the overall picture. But for this book I have set aside some of my natural enthusiasm for resort timesharing and relied on my solid business experience to provide you, I think quite objectively, with the pros and cons of the new concept. Moreover, I have tried to help you make intelligent decisions about resort timesharing not only by describing these pros and cons from the buyer's point of view, but also by showing you the *other* side of timesharing, through the viewpoints of salespeople and brokers as well. I want you to judge for yourself if resort timesharing makes sense for your family. But whatever you decide, you will be able to make up your mind with a clear understanding of what timesharing actually is.

It is my hope that this book will accelerate public understanding and focus attention on what just may be the private sector's answer to beating the vacation-inflation game. Perhaps the wheels of government will eventually grind inflation to a halt, or at least slow it to a respectable trickle; in the meantime, each family has to find its own solution. You still have the last say in how you spend your money, and we have the ability to test and prove new products in the marketplace. So I think that if you consider your own vacation preferences and limitations and use the information provided in this book, you will view the vacation-inflation-beating strategy of timesharing with as much optimism as I do.

CHAPTER 1

How Resort Timesharing Works

WHAT IS RESORT TIMESHARING?

If someone were to offer you a fully-furnished luxury condominium valued at $150,000, overlooking the ocean or near a ski slope, for $6,000, would you buy it? If the seller threw into the bargain the opportunity for you to use his other vacation home in the Alps, or in Las Vegas, or in Mexico, would you be tempted to accept?

One experienced traveler might snap up the deal. Another, less informed, might say, "What's the catch? It sounds too good to be true!"

What you have been offered is *interval resort timesharing*, the hottest innovation in real estate to reach the consumer in this decade, and by far the most talked-about property deal since the advent of the condominium.

Resort timesharing is simply the purchase of a luxurious vacation home in increments of a week or more by a number of buyers, each of whom buy only the time which they will use each year. Because the expense of owning and operating a vacation home is then divided among its

11

many users, the cost to each is only a small fraction of what a vacation home would otherwise cost. Thus, families who may have been squeezed out of the vacation-home market by spiraling inflation, and those who may never even have considered themselves able to buy one, can now afford to live like the rich.

By the end of 1980, more than 400,000 families had chosen to participate in this new concept in over 600 resorts around the world. With new resorts continually being added to the marketplace, it is estimated that the number of families purchasing interval vacations is climbing to the rate of 5,000 *per week*. And despite a few problems in the early stages of this development (which we'll discuss later in this book), one notable factor during the first five years of timesharing's growth has been the remarkable lack of complaints to government or media about "ripoffs."

Resort timesharing is marketed under various names that represent a particular form of the concept: *interval ownership, right-to-use, vacation lease, vacation license* and *club membership*. The terms most often used are *resort timesharing* (shortened to *timesharing*) and *interval resort sharing*; the former was derived from the already established idea of companies sharing expensive computers; the latter definition is more recent and perhaps more indicative of what the concept is all about.

Generally speaking, each type is designed to provide a family with accommodations superior to most vacation hotels and motels and with the use of standard or expanded recreation facilities for a specified number of years. The purchase guarantees accommodations for future vacations at today's prices, or "freezes" the cost of lodgings at the one-time price for the duration of the purchase agreement. Interval resort sharing is less expensive, *on a cumulative basis*, than renting accommodations over a period of years—regardless of inflation. The difference in cost between ongoing rentals and interval resort sharing will become even greater in the face of continued inflation, since rentals will reflect the rising costs passed on to the consumer by the motel owner. So the timesharing one-time cost for accommodations becomes a hedge against inflation since it cannot be escalated. Although it sounds simple enough, it becomes more complicated when you consider the various types of timesharing being sold by developers. Some offer "ownership" along the lines of a condominium purchase, while others offer "right-to-use" along the lines of a vacation membership club. Each is covered in greater depth in the next chapter.

Sound like a good idea? It *is*, and the proof lies in its almost worldwide success. Are you wondering why it has been such a well-kept secret? Perhaps you've just breezed by the articles in all the major newspapers and magazines, or missed the TV coverage. However, by the time you finish this book, you will know almost everything about timesharing, and you should be able to judge if it really is "too good to be true."

HOW DOES IT WORK?

The rental inflation charts on pages 15–17 illustrate the major advantage of resort timesharing over rentals, which leave you with nothing except several years' worth of rent receipts. Resort timesharing becomes much less expensive over the long term because the developer sets a one-time fee which, unlike yearly rentals, will not change over the time period of the contract.

But before dissecting the financial aspects of timesharing, let's look at how a resort becomes a timeshare entity. First, either a condominium or a leasehold is established in a prime area. It might be an existing motel, hotel, apartment complex or condominium, or it might also be a piece of unimproved property upon which a new resort complex will be built. The total number of dwelling units in the resort is then multiplied by the 52 weeks in the annual calendar; this provides the total number of "unit weeks" which can be sold at the resort—after deducting the number of weeks per year that the developer sets aside as maintenance weeks (those weeks each year that will never have occupancy in order to allow major cleaning and refurbishing to keep the apartments in "like new" condition). Some resorts establish two different weeks in the annual calendar for maintenance (usually in the fall and spring) if extreme weather or other circumstances place unusual wear and tear on the apartments. Ski resorts usually fall into this category—carpets may require cleaning before and after the snow season. Most resorts, however, need only set aside one week for heavy annual maintenance. Thus, 51 weeks are offered for sale in each apartment. A 40-unit resort would then have a total of 2,040 unit weeks available for sale. This means that the maximum number of potential families who will "share" this resort as co-owners or as members will be 2,040.

Although 2,040 families sounds like a logistical nightmare, it really isn't. Most buyers tend to purchase more than one week because they are entitled to two or more weeks of vacation each year. Obviously, these numbers will vary at each resort, with the number of participants decreasing as the average number of weeks purchased increases. For example, if each family purchases two weeks, there will be 1,020 participants; if the average number of weeks purchased is 1.5 (some buy one, others buy more), there will be 1,530 participants.

Bear in mind that you will never see all of these people. Since there are only 40 units in the resort, only 40 families can occupy the accommodations during one week. And developers are careful in restricting the number of people in each unit, based on maintaining a reasonable ratio of people to the number of bedrooms and overall square footage of the unit.

The rule of thumb on occupancy is two people per bedroom and two for each den or living room that provides a convertible couch. A two-bedroom apartment should be comfortable for six people if the convertible

WHAT HAPPENS TO VACATION RENTALS AS INFLATION COMPOUNDS 10% PER YEAR.

	DAILY AVERAGE ROOM RATE	10% INCREASE NEW ROOM RATE	TOTAL 7 DAY VACATION	CUMULATIVE TOTAL IN YEARS	NUMBER OF YEARS
1979	$ 50.	$ 55.	$ 385.	$ 385.	1.
1980	55.	60.	420.	805.	2.
1981	60.	66.	462.	1,267.	3.
1982	66.	72.	504.	1 771.	4.
1983	72.	79.	553.	2,324.	5.
1984	79.	86.	602.	2,926.	6.
1985	86.	94.	658.	3,584.	7.
1986	94.	103.	721.	4,305.	8.
1987	103.	113.	791.	5,096.	9.
1988	113.	124.	868.	5,964.	10.
1989	124.	136.	952.	6,916.	11.
1990	136.	149.	1,043.	7,959.	12.
1991	149.	163.	1,141.	9,100.	13.
1992	163.	179.	1,253.	10,353.	14.
1993	179.	196.	1,372.	11,725.	15.
1994	196.	215.	1,505.	13,230.	16.
1995	215.	236.	1,652.	14,882.	17.
1996	236.	259.	1,813.	16,695.	18.
1997	259.	284.	1,988.	18,683.	19.
1998	284.	312.	2,184.	20,867.	20.
1999	312.	343.	2,401.	23,268.	21.
2000	343.	377.	2,639.	25,907.	22.

ABOVE FIGURES DO NOT INCLUDE MISCELLANEOUS PENNIES DELETED FOR SIMPLICITY.

Projection of Future Daily Rates for Resort Hotels ★

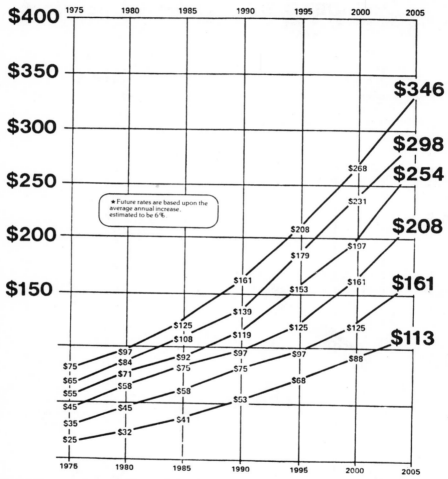

★ Future rates are based upon the average annual increase, estimated to be 6%.

*Permission to reprint this material, which originally appeared in MOTOR INN JOURNAL, is granted by special permission of the copyright holders, Harcourt Brace Jovanovich Inc.

Inflation & our rising vacation costs -

"RESORT DEVELOPMENT TODAY"
A NATIONAL RESORT MAGAZINE STATED

"Hotel rates are averaging a 10% rise annually. This means that by 1984 a vacationing family will be paying nearly twice as much for resort lodging as they paid for the same lodging in 1977. Moreover, the outlook is for hotel rates to rise faster than general inflation."

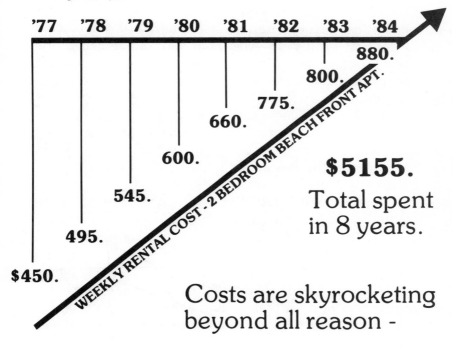

'77 '78 '79 '80 '81 '82 '83 '84

880.

800.

775.

660.

600.

545.

495.

$450.

WEEKLY RENTAL COST - 2 BEDROOM BEACH FRONT APT.

$5155.
Total spent in 8 years.

Costs are skyrocketing beyond all reason -

couch is double or queen-size; a three-bedroom unit would accommodate eight people under the same circumstances and a one-bedroom will handle up to four people.

What we are arriving at is an optimum use of prime vacation space by the largest possible number of people —without sacrificing anyone's comfort or use of resort facilities—over a year's period of time.

Think about this key point for a minute.

What a resort timeshare developer is doing is what all motel/hotel operators would like to accomplish—the 100 percent occupancy of all available units for 100 percent of the time each year—year after year. Since part of the price you pay for the daily rental of a motel room must cover the ongoing motel costs when it has *vacancies* (insurance, utilities, taxes, depreciation of facilities and materials, and base personnel salaries must be costed into room rates on a 365-day basis), you are paying a premium in order to assure the motel a profit. Now, this is not to say that motel rooms at certain times of the year aren't a bargain or rented out for less profit (or on a break-even basis); motels will often opt for slimmer margins of profit in the "off season" in order to cover operating expenses until their profits climb from "in-season" rates and fuller capacity. The airlines work the same way. "In season," they don't have to give anything away. "Off season," they advertise extra special-saver fares in order to maximize occupancy on each flight. Their saleable inventory, too, is time and space; they can never recapture the revenues lost from the flight that just left the ground half full. Nor can a motel recapture the revenues lost from too many vacancies last week.

If a motel could book all its rooms a year in advance, year after year, it would make a tremendous profit. But there would be no vacancies for those businessmen or tourists who stop by for a night or two—until someone down the street offered lower rates. Or until the owners discounted room rates enough to ensure maximum capacity for the longest period of time. The consumer would then get better value, and the motel would meet its financial objectives through greater occupancy even though the nightly profit per room was less. This is what resort timesharing is all about and how it works. It packages a long-term occupancy agreement for each family and rewards the buyer with a set rate that cannot change during the length of the agreement. Rental operators may try to guarantee low rates for a year or two—perhaps up to three years—but inevitably the costs of competition and inflation will be passed on to the renter. The marketing costs required to maintain high occupancy levels are expensive! Some motels, unable to solve this dilemma, go broke. Some struggle by. Some, however, are extremely successful, and we'll take a look at them in a later chapter. Others have investigated interval resort sharing and moved into the industry in order to eliminate problems of vacancy and ongoing promotion expenses.

IS IT A FAD OR FOR REAL?

Resort timesharing is the "new kid on the block." It is quite a new alternative to the old vacation plan. Some of the best people in real estate, law and finance have studied meticulously the intricacies of this timeshare concept. Today, leaders in these and other fields continue to scrutinize its economic and sociological impact, with an optimistic eye on its growth potential.

An industry conference in the spring of 1981 revealed that resort timesharing has begun to attract wealthy but conservative entrepreneurs—those who usually appear only when a new real estate idea has proven itself; who, for example, waited until the condominium concept had become well-enough established to merit their investments. This infusion of sophisticated business leaders will enable resort timesharing to grow still further and to function at the highest levels of American business.

Moving into the picture are such companies as Chase Manhattan Bank, Citibank of New York, Barclay's American Business Credit (a division of England's Barclay's Bank), the Bank of California, Greyhound Real Estate Corporation and the Hotel and Restaurant Management Department of Cornell University. Already participating are such giants as the Mellon Bank, Columbia University, Security Pacific Finance Corporation, General Electric Credit Corporation, Dial Financial Corporation and a number of prestigious law firms.

Some of the major stock brokerage houses have expanded into real estate and are investigating the viability of resort sharing. In Canada, the concept has been warmly received by major banks who cover all ten provinces and handle consumer loans for interval purchases as they would auto or personal loans.

The growth of the concept, since it was first introduced in North America in 1975, indicates that interval resort sharing has moved from the fad stage to the "for real" stage. Analysts estimate that there are 31 million North American families who vacation annually and can afford the cost of one or more unit weeks. Not all of these 31 million will buy into timesharing, of course, but the numbers, when considered with the early success of resort sales in key vacation areas, are impressive. Entrepreneurs are entering the field rapidly, producing a ripple effect in real estate and motel circles.

With its spread to all major resort areas and the subsequent benefits enjoyed by developers and hotel owners through full occupancy, interval resort sharing has begun to appeal to even the toughest skeptics. And why not? Considering that the average unit week sold for about $6,000 in 1981, the potential market adds up to $186 billion—huge figures and enough sales potential to attract anybody's attention! And if the average sale were 1.5 weeks—add half again as much dollar volume, mindful, too, that the average price may be even higher in the years ahead when the concept becomes a household word.

HOW IT BEGAN AND GREW

Although Americans were unprepared initially for the condominium concept—that of sharing the ownership of one apartment building—they soon accepted the idea that it was no longer necessary to have tree-shaded streets and a vegetable garden to enjoy the benefits of real estate ownership. Condominiums gained popularity, and millions more people were able to own their piece of "land."

An interesting fact about those first condos is that they were mostly located in the country's resort areas. The units were second homes. Because they were empty for a good part of each year, some innovative developers began to market their buildings on a rental pool basis. That is, owners held the deed to the apartment, but management would rent it out for them to help owners recoup at least part of their costs. The progression from full-ownership condominiums to rental pools set the stage nicely for the introduction of resort sharing. The illustrations on pages 22 and 23 will help you visualize the concept.

The very first interval resort sharing is said to have started in 1964, however, at Superdevolvy, a ski resort in the French Alps where multiple ownership of dwelling units brought certainty of confirmed reservations to ski buffs who yearned for a place of their own. In 1968, the Paris-based Club Hotel entered the field and has since converted more than 20 resort properties into the interval concept, in partnership with the well-known Club Med.

The Europeans, however, seem to credit American ingenuity with really establishing the concept and bringing it to public attention. The U.S. and European resorts that developed in those early stages were sold via "right-to-use," where the buyer actually leased the apartment on a weekly basis for a set period of time. In the early 1970s a Miami company, Caribbean International Corporation, converted three faltering condominium projects in St. Thomas, Fort Lauderdale and Puerto Rico to timesharing. But the energy and economic crunch of the mid-70s

Interval Ownership. It merely breaks resort home ownership down into smaller, more affordable segments.

REAL ESTATE DIMENSION #1.
LENGTH & WIDTH

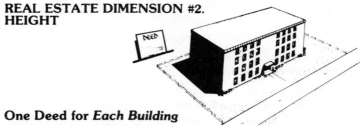

One Deed for *Each Piece of Land*

Historically, private real estate ownership is a recent phenomenon. In Europe, it did not extend to the masses until after the Revolutionary War. In the early 1700's, settlers brought to N. America the British recorded Deed system to show ownership — measured via metes and bounds (measuring length and width by feet) with no pressing need to consider height.

REAL ESTATE DIMENSION #2.
HEIGHT

One Deed for *Each Building*

As land became filled, socio-economic impetus created the next dimension . . . height. Taller buildings became a prominent feature with the advent of improved engineering and materials. Still, only one Deed was needed to show ownership of the real estate — such as the 8 unit apartment building used in this illustration.

REAL ESTATE DIMENSION #3.
CONDOMINIUM

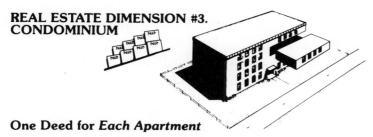

One Deed for *Each Apartment*

The convenience of apartment living and the tax benefits of home ownership created the 3rd dimension of real estate. Condominium evolution allowed for as many Deeds (on one piece of Property) as there were living units.

Thus, ownership of this example apartment building (and facilities) is now jointly in the hands of 8 individuals — each with a Deed.

REAL ESTATE DIMENSION #4.
INTERVAL OWNERSHIP

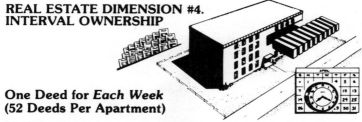

One Deed for *Each Week*
(52 Deeds Per Apartment)

TIME becomes the new dimension to its predecessors. It merely extends Einstein's observation to real estate ownership. Now, the Deed shows ownership for the apartment on a weekly time interval — permitting the owner's use only to the week specified on the Deed.

Ingenuity has propelled man into being able to control vacation home ownership, bringing it back into affordable range of everyone. With the same inherent practicality as home ownership.

23

forced cessation of sales, although current members still have access to their resort facilities and accommodations. These were times when a large number of condominium developers were caught out on a limb. Florida, for instance, was glutted with nearly completed but still unsold condominiums. The real estate investment trusts, once a seemingly endless source for consumer financing, were staggering toward their court-appointed reorganizations; savings and loan associations were pulling back their horns and builders couldn't find financing at marketable rates for the dwindling number of interested buyers. There couldn't have been a worse time to present a new vacation concept. The right idea had come along at the wrong time in a business where timing is everything. The end result was some dramatic failures in an industry just emerging from its embryonic stage.

But good ideas have a way of surviving, and timesharing was soon to appear again—this time to stay and grow to its present impressive proportions. With condominiums escalating in price, as developers and mortgagors sought to recapture their investments, a major segment of the buying public had finally given up on the dream of a second home at the beach or in the mountains. And while the wealthy have always had the opportunity to own vacation homes, many of them as well were forced to defray costs by renting the second house to others when it would be vacant. In addition to bringing in some extra cash, rentals enabled owners to cut their taxes because they could deduct their entire maintenance expenses. However, in the 1960s, Congress partially closed this loophole and limited tax deductions—a move which played a role in substantially reducing the demand for second homes.

The exorbitant inflation rates experienced in this country over the last decade have pushed housing costs out of reach and second homes out of the budget of thousands of families.

Now the timing was right for a commonsense answer

to the problem. Two resorts in Florida decided to run the risk despite an uninformed public, leery financial institutions and a press eager to dredge up past failures; they were Hawk's Nest of Marathon, in the Florida Keys, and Sanibel Beach Club, on southwest Florida's famed shelling beaches of Sanibel Island. According to Mark Langer, a Miami attorney specializing in resort sharing, these two resorts were the first to be marketed, sold out and turned over to their owners' association by their developers. Thus, after ten years of financial and conceptual alterations, the new concept was reborn and ready to go. As new resorts appeared on the scene from Florida to Mexico and Hawaii, many developers followed the American innovation of providing deeded ownership for each week. From the right-to-use membership plan devised in Europe came the interval-ownership alternative from the U.S. The concept took on a new dimension, and today both forms are offered around the globe.

While some industry observers suggest that timesharing was forced by overbuilding of condominiums in 1974–75 in a depressed market, in fact very few developers actually converted to resort sharing at that time. Whether due to skepticism or lack of information about the new concept, most chose to hold onto their condominium developments until better times.

Today, resorts can be found in all major vacation areas from the ski slopes of Colorado, Montana, Vermont and New Hampshire to the sunny beaches of Florida, Mexico, Hawaii and California. Guided by the preferences of American vacationers, developers have rushed to meet the growing demand to establish resorts in the favored tourist areas, and resort sharing is now widely available. In fact, most states have at least one interval resort, and many have dozens. From Hilton Head to Gatlinburg, from Atlantic City to New York, from New Orleans to Las Vegas, interval resort vacations are now a part of family life for over 200,000 U.S. families—half of the world's interval-owning population. And in Canada, thought to be the most vacation-travel-oriented country per capita in the world, the boom is just starting. Resorts have sprung up in Quebec, Ontario, Manitoba and British Columbia—with more planned in all provinces.

Interval resort sharing, then, is hardly a fad. While there are disadvantages and pitfalls which we will cover later in this chapter, the consensus is that the concept is free of most "bugs" and has tremendous potential—especially when you consider that the consumer can travel to affiliated resorts around the world practically rent free.

THE EXCHANGE PROGRAM: A TIMELY ALTERNATIVE

During the early days, one of the biggest objections to buying resort timesharing was voiced by the question: "What if I can't take my vacation at the same time every year?" Another question asked was, "What if I'm transferred in my job or don't want to vacation at the same place year after year?" In those days there were no answers, and both buyers and salespeople wished someone would find a solution to these problems.

Someone eventually did. And it was so simple.

At the time condominium sales were plummeting in the United States, an exchange network emerged, operated by an independent company whose sole objective was to handle exchanges between resort members seeking location and time flexibility.

One of the "bugs" in the original concept had been worked out, and interval resort buyers were provided with an exciting new dimension in timesharing. Resort Condominiums International (RCI) designed a program to list and facilitate exchange requests between participating resorts; like a travel club, RCI simply kept track of who wanted to go where and then handled the paperwork for a nominal fee when each trade was confirmed.

The concept of interval resort sharing had now come of age, and the public response improved markedly.

ADVANTAGES AND LIMITATIONS OF RESORT TIMESHARING

Subsequent chapters will discuss more fully details you can expect to encounter in becoming a buyer of interval resort sharing. We have capsulized the concept as follows:

Advantages

1. Through resort sharing, you can be guaranteed the use of a specific apartment or motel suite in a resort area of your choice for one week or more —for just the amount of time each year that makes sense for you and your family.
2. You can budget your cost of accommodations at the amortized weekly breakout of your purchase price, divided by the number of weeks covered in your purchase agreement. Because you pay or contract for it at the stated price, it can never increase.
3. You avoid the hassles of worrying about early reservations and the possibility of hearing at the front desk, "Sorry, we've no record of your reservations and we're booked solid."
4. You can let others—anyone you wish—use your apartment or suite, simply by notifying resort management a little ahead of time.
5. You can rent your unit, either acting as your own landlord or using the services of a rental agent or other associate.
6. In many resorts, you can sell your "share" at any time, for any price, to virtually anyone you wish. Or you can commission an agent to do so for you.
7. You can bequeath your "share" in your estate, like any other asset, to anyone you wish.
8. You can exchange your vacation weeks, depending on availability and membership rules, for vacations in any affiliated resort, with only a

nominal exchange fee for confirmed reservations.

9. You can enjoy most resort facilities without charge, as an owner or member of the club (golf, skiing, etc., may be offered to resort residents at special rates).

10. You can make new friends with other interval residents who have similar interests; you'll see many of the same people each year and develop a sense of community seldom found otherwise.

11. You will be more likely to take that necessary break from your busy schedule when your vacation has been "prearranged," and that could turn out to be the best medicine your doctor could prescribe for you (or your family).

12. Your accommodations will probably provide a luxury you hadn't thought you could afford. No longer will you have to suffer overcrowding or motel mediocrity. Your apartment will be fully furnished and equipped, ready to be your home away from home.

13. In most cases, you will be able to fix some or all of your meals at your "home" resort; the convenience and savings will be significant. (Restaurants, too, are victims of inflationary spirals.)

14. Maid service is an option at most resorts; you can do your own light housework, or you can have daily maid service on a cost basis by merely telling management in advance to plan it for you.

15. In resorts that provide member or owner associations, the effect of inflation on your management fees will be kept under control by your membership association. You'll have a voice, or proxy vote via directors, in preventive or remedial action against inflationary impact.

16. Your reduced cost for annual vacations should soon result in considerable savings over comparable rented accommodations.

17. Your vacations are virtually worry-free; manage-

ment takes care of all maintenance chores before, during and after your visit.

18. Replacement of furnishings and equipment is provided for in the annual maintenance fee; there is no heavy burden on any one member, since expenses are spread out over all "sharers" of the unit.

Limitations

The greatest possibilities for error in timesharing lie in your decision about resort selection, unit size, calendar period or in misjudging your preferred vacation lifestyle. For example:

1. You may prefer the privacy of a smaller resort or a separate vacation home.
2. The recreational facilities and other resort amenities that will be a part of your financial maintenance responsibilities may not be of interest to you—simply may not fit your personal needs.
3. The budget for annual maintenance could be grossly understated to promote sales and could quickly become too expensive for you.
4. It's unlikely, but the developer *could* go broke. Be *sure* there's a provision for refund or full occupancy rights equal to your purchase.
5. You may have difficulty arranging to exchange your time unit with another resort if your time period does not occur during a peak season.
6. You cannot furnish or redecorate the apartment to your taste.
7. If you are used to vacationing for six to eight weeks per year at a condominium or lakeside second home, timesharing is probably not for you.

If you don't take precautions and use some of the guidelines covered in this book, you could wind up a loser. Any business which has the potential to soar into a multibillion-dollar industry in just a few years is bound to attract a few charlatans and the occasional incompetent; fortunately, the industry and many states have formulated consumer protection guidelines which discourage shoddy operations.

Should your review of a resort's potential not measure up to the guidelines in this book, proceed with caution. But if you find a resort which meets your standards and budget, you may lose out on a good value if you "kick the tires" too long. Most resorts have honest sales representatives; most developers are adequately financed and retain knowledgeable, capable management; most resorts can fulfill your vacation expectations—if you know what to look for and if you know what questions to ask.

Advantages of Resort Sharing

Sell it Like Any Asset

New Friendships

Loan it to Friends & Relations

Equity $ Position

Ample Resort Facilities

Guaranteed Vacation

Belong to a Special Group

Use it without Reservations

Worry-Free Vacations

Rent It Out

Freeze Costs of Future Vacations

Establish Children's Lifestyle

Bequeath to Heirs

Exchange for New Places

Ownership with Deed & Title

Luxuriously Furnished & Equipped

Potential Appreciation

Have a Voice in Vacation Quality

Accommodations that beat Motel Mediocrity

Improve Your Vacation Lifestyle

Limitations of Resort Sharing

- You can't take home the TV sets, towels or games.
- No pets (they deserve a vacation from you, too).
- You can't break things up without paying for them.*
- You can't repaper the walls in your favorite prints.
- You are responsible for a share of the annual maintenance just like any real estate equity (but some are tax deductible).
- It's unlikely, but the developer could go broke. Be sure there's a provision for refund or full occupancy rights equal to your purchase.
- You may have difficulty arranging to exchange your time unit with another resort if your time period does not occur during peak season.
- If you prefer the privacy of a separate vacation home, or if you are used to vacationing 6–8 weeks per year at a condominium or lakeside home, timesharing is probably not for you.

* No charge for normal wear and tear; periodic replacement of furnishings and appliances is included, as are insurance, utilities, management, etc. Your share is split equally with all the other vacation partners to greatly reduce the individual cost.

2

Understanding the Different Forms of Timesharing

There are several different types of interval resort offerings. Each has its own unique advantages; some have a few minor drawbacks. One type may suit your needs better than another. Keep in mind that many resorts do not specify clearly in their brochures what type of interval they are offering; most have a tendency to call their program "resort timesharing" or "interval resort sharing," which is the name of the concept rather than the actual type they offer.

Of the several kinds of interval resorts, there are two basic types: *ownership* and *right-to-use*. Generally speaking, ownership provides an equity interest in the resort similar to home or condominium ownership, complete with a deed filed at the county courthouse. Right-to-use is, as the name applies, a nonequity ownership position and simply provides you with an occupancy membership in the resort for the specified number of years in the agreement. You'll need to know more details about how the two types vary in order to decide which type of timesharing is best for you. Since the programs differ because of location or legal requirements, both types won't always be available as developers opt for the type that more easily fits local requirements.

RIGHT-TO-USE

This form of resort sharing does not offer ownership of any material assets of the resort. It simply offers you occupancy or right-to-use vacation accommodations and resort facilities on a weekly basis for a number of years—as few as ten years or as many as 99 years. At the expiration of the term, the occupancy rights revert to the resort owner or club for disposition as they see fit. Some plans offer you the option to renew participation at expiration, for either the original price or a fee beneficial to you and the owner. In this manner, you might enjoy a ten-year vacation program for $3,000 and extend it for another ten years at the inflation-fighting renewal fee of $3,000. You can see the advantages of controlling vacation costs for 20 years at $6,000 if this option is included in your agreement. Inflation could make the renewal option very attractive in the years ahead.

There are several reasons why some resorts are made available only on a right-to-use basis. There may be so many apartments in a building that the developer faces heavy legal and financial burdens in partitioning for individual ownership. He may prefer to offer only a portion of the building for right-to-use and keep the balance for rental operations. If it were a condominium, not a time-sharing property, the developer would have to partition *all* units and all the physical parts of the building in order to assign legal protection and liabilities on an equal basis to the individual buyers.

Local ordinances or federal law may preclude outright ownership; Mexico, for instance, prohibits land ownership by non-nationals in many coastal areas. Ireland permits only leases on property, though they may extend to 99 years and therefore be as attractive as ownership.

The developer may wish to retain ownership of the property and make other plans for it at the expiration of its interval use.

From your point of view, right-to-use has both positive and negative features. As a non-owner, you are not building any equity in your investment. And you will have no voice in management and maintenance operations, especially in the controls used to combat inflation in the maintenance fees which you pay. There will be no restrictions on the sale of the resort during your term of use, nor will you have a choice as to the buyer. You may be restricted from reselling your unit weeks or limited to the amount of your original purchase price as developers seek to avoid violating the restrictions of the Securities and Exchange Commission (SEC) and to curb investment speculation presentations by sales personnel. Because a right-to-use unit is not classified as a real estate transaction, resort sales personnel are not required to be licensed in real estate in many states and countries. Sales presentations, therefore, are to be taken at face value; you should make your decision based on what you see in print.

Right-to-use sets a limit on your participation, and the value of your investment may depreciate in proportion to the number of years left on the use agreement. For example, a 20-year program could be worth 50 percent or less of the amount you paid after ten years of use, although inflation and popularity of your resort may help to raise the value of your unit. Let's say you paid $4,000 for a 20-year program and used it for ten years; another buyer may not be willing to pay $2,000 for the remaining ten years. On the other hand, inflation could shoot similar vacation units into the $500-per-week rental bracket, and your buyer would benefit by paying even up to the original $4,000, still beating the $5,000 he may have to pay out for rentals in the next ten years.

On the positive side, you may prefer not to become

involved in the mechanics and responsibilities of ownership. Right-to-use units are usually less expensive; you will probably have possession for fewer years than if you were buying outright; and because the owner retains title to the property, he can be competitive when establishing original prices as well as renewal prices at the end of your term.

Because occupancy rights revert back to the developer, he has a vested interest in keeping the property in top shape. He will want your renewal, or an opportunity for a good resale.

In most right-to-use developments, the management operation will be in experienced and responsible hands, eliminating the necessity of your being involved in areas not familiar to you. Most maintenance budgets are established with a ceiling on the possible annual increases to members, and this ceiling is usually based on the Consumer Cost of Living Index issued monthly by the U.S. Department of Labor. For your protection if the resort is sold, your original agreement should state clearly your right to use the resort for the time remaining in your contract. Any change of ownership can be to your advantage. A "changing of the guard" may result in new benefits or much improved operations.

The paperwork is simpler under right-to-use and, therefore, closing costs and legal fees are less. You simply pay your money, get your certificate of occupancy for your time period for the number of years offered and that's it. Maintenance charges will be the only fee to vary each year, and even their increases should be slight under competent management.

INTERVAL OWNERSHIP

This is the most widely used and popular type of equity ownership. It is, in fact, a two-part arrangement, but does not require separate documentation to cover the transition from the first step to the second.

Estate for Years The first part is called an *estate for years*. This establishes ownership of the unit for a set number of years estimated to be the useful life of the building (usually 40 years). At the end of that period, the second part kicks in: all buyers automatically become "tenants in common" in the ownership of the resort. This undivided share in the resort and common property is usually based on each individual's number of weeks previously owned.

Time Span Ownership A less frequently used type of interval ownership, *time span ownership* (TSO), is based on the tenancy-in-common idea from the beginning. The buyer receives an undivided interest in the whole living unit, based pro rata on the number of weeks selected, but is not given direct priority interest in any specified time period (which is established by a separate legal agreement).

Cooperative In areas like New York which do not recognize the condominium structure, the *cooperative* approach to interval ownership is emerging. Buyers receive ownership shares similar to stock in the overall property. They can select a specific week and building (or apartment) with ownership distribution similar to tenancy in common.

The certificates or deeds and title insurance provide timeshare buyers all the protection they'll need. As owners, they can rent, sell or bequeath their interest as they would any other asset. They pay property taxes and can deduct interest and taxes on their prorated share from their income tax.

In both ownership and right-to-use timesharing, you will be responsible for annual maintenance fees, just as you are in your own home. The rights of occupancy carry the obligations of protecting the property offered. Somehow, when a condominium is involved, people balk at paying an annual fee for that nebulous term, "maintenance." A close look at exactly what's covered should convince even the most skeptical buyer it's a reasonable and just assessment.

Maintenance is essential because it *protects your investment!* Just as your car retains its value longer if you take good care of it, your vacation apartment retains its value over the years through careful maintenance. But you don't carry the whole burden. The cost is shared equally by everyone who has a share in your apartment and your portion is thereby significantly smaller than if this responsibility were solely yours.

VACATION LICENSES, LEASES AND MEMBERSHIPS

Right-to-use is offered in several different formats, but all are quite similar.

The *vacation license* gives the buyer the right to use a selected unit for either a number of floating weeks over the duration or a specified week for a number of years or for the useful life of the building. The buyer is usually free to sell his license but more often is restricted from doing so at a profit. He may also be restricted from renting. These restrictions are intended to prevent the license from being interpreted as a security under the federal and state securities laws by assuring that the buyer is purchasing only for his use and enjoyment.

The *vacation lease* is similar to the license in that the buyer has a lease on a particular unit and a fixed occupancy period. The lease, however, is transferable and rentals are more commonly acceptable.

The *club membership* provides the right to occupy a unit for a fixed period each year. The club, a nonprofit association similar to a country club, purchases or leases a building or group of buildings for the benefits of club members. The time period may be fixed or floating on an annual basis.

FIXED AND FLOATING WEEKS

The most common system for interval vacation selection is by *fixed week*—where you select one or more specific weeks on the calendar and the contract declares you to be the only legal occupant for those time periods. The developer is giving you the exclusive right to occupy a specific unit for a set, or fixed, week annually. Even if you elect not to use, rent or trade your week, management will respect the privacy of your unit just as if you were there, since you are responsible for the maintenance and contents at that time.

If your resort provides you with an equity position vis-à-vis interval ownership, fixed week is the most common transferral of that ownership. The weeks you buy will be stated specifically on your deed by number (example: "Palmetto Dunes Resort, Unit 307, weeks 6 and 7") as legal proof of partitionment to you as owner.

The other system sometimes offered is called a *floating week*. In this system you purchase within a season or price range (rather than a fixed-week selection) and have an occupancy right within those ranges annually on a first-reservation, first-confirmation base.

And unlike hotels that often overbook, the developer can't sell more than the total number of weeks available in each range.

You can buy "summer" and have your pick of any of the 13 weeks in June, July and August as long as the one you pick is not already reserved. Or you can pick "spring-fall," which are often similar in price and popularity, and reserve a week's vacation in your choice of either season on an availability basis.

This system is most often used under the right-to-use programs, since there is no deed involved. It is possible, however, to use this system in an ownership resort under unique applications of real estate law. A cooperative could provide joint ownership in common with all the other buyers and create a "company" effect that served its shareholders on a first-come, first-served, or floating-reservation, basis.

The pros and cons in selecting either the fixed or floating systems are fairly clear. The fixed week gives you assurance that you can always count on accommodations at the time you've selected; you can expedite rentals and exchanges faster by already having your unit week confirmed to relay on to the exchange network, your rental agent or customer. The peace of mind alone may make this more beneficial to you.

The floating-week system allows greater flexibility and seasonal variety. For example, your neighbors will seldom be the same each year. On the other hand, the floating week involves more paperwork and less certainty that you will get the time you request. The longer you wait, the less favorable the time or unit may be for you, unless your vacation dates are flexible. Holidays and prime season weeks will generate the biggest demand and thereby the greatest difficulty in securing the date you want.

The preference for either will become a matter of personal convenience, unless there is only one system available from the resort you select.

OTHER VACATION ALTERNATIVES

Even with the conversion of a great number of hotels and motels in prime vacation locations, there always will be those that choose to rent their accommodations to the public by the day, month and season. And the more motels that convert to interval make it that much better and less competitive for those who don't. True, the demand for the diminished supply of rental accommodations will increase, and reservation hassles will be much more of a problem, but you'll be able to find a room at the inn if you plan in advance.

One interesting revelation about rental accommodations is that although few motels are being built in prime locations these days by anyone other than the giants, luxury hotels have shown new growth potential. The big names in the industry (Hilton, Sheraton, Holiday Inns, etc.) have recently built some skyscrapers to accommodate not only vacationers but corporate travelers and business meetings. Expense accounts are more liberal than the average guy's budget, and the hotels can (and must) place a premium on their more plush suites and facilities when catering to businesses. As companies combine business with pleasure, hotel resorts on the ocean provide the best accommodations when price is less important than the company image. Vacationers can now enjoy these same luxuries and facilities; the only inequality is in the price—companies get special group rates while the vacationer pays the high individual rate.

If you have good connections with a realtor or rental agent and don't care for a resort atmosphere, you can still find some unique vacation homes or cottages. Obviously, you'll pay more for them in peak seasons, but you may be able to arrange your own timeshare agreement with the owner to reserve the place for a few years in advance. Or you can become an important customer for owners of resort timeshare units who put them up for rent. As the number of buyers in the interval concept keeps growing, so will the amount of available rental units. If what you want is luxurious accommodations once in a while, the interval rental market is an obvious answer. If you have a friend who owns some available weeks, you may be able to arrange to rent some of his time.

There will always be a certain percentage of the public that doesn't want anything less than the whole pie—owning or renting by the slice has little appeal. For them full ownership of a second home or resort condominium is still the best arrangement.

Condominiums and second homes have not lost their attractiveness, but they have become too expensive for most of us. The problem with owning the whole pie is

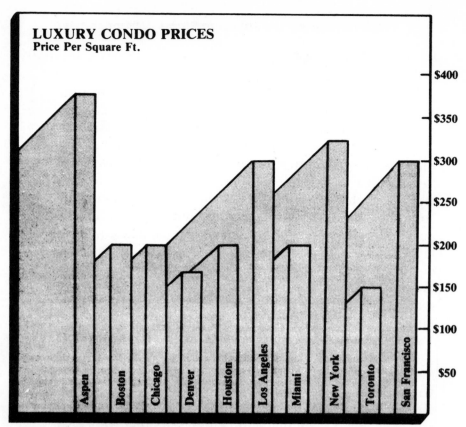

LUXURY CONDO PRICES
Price Per Square Ft.

Bars (left to right): Aspen, Boston, Chicago, Denver, Houston, Los Angeles, Miami, New York, Toronto, San Francisco

$300 Per Square Foot:
Luxury Condo Prices Skyrocket *

Luxury condominium prices are topping $300 per square foot in major markets in the U.S. such as New York, Los Angeles and San Francisco. And in the fashionable resort of Aspen Colorado, prices are nearing the $400 per square foot mark.

But, a recent U.S. study predicts prices will slown down after the rapid, 100 per cent increases in the past few years. It says the current, high price levels for luxury condominiums are caused by:

• Overseas purchasers who have accounted for more than 60 per cent of recent sales, thus increasing the demand for luxury condominiums.

• Rapidly rising construction and financing costs.

• The rapidly decreasing amount of rental space available.

• Government restrictions which increase the risk of conversion.

The study predicts general price slowdown in the luxury condominium market because people will not be able to afford such expensive housing. It predicts a surge of conversion of desirable property from rental to condominium in urban centers and new condominium construction dominating major markets such as New York and Miami.

In Canada it is being predicted that Montreal, Toronto and Calgary will experience the luxury condominium boom for at least the next few years.

42

*Courtesy, *The Condominium*, January 1981.

simply one of dollars and cents. The average second home is used only 17 days a year, along with perhaps a few holiday weekends, although if you plan to use your second home for retirement or as an investment, you can certainly justify an expenditure of $80,000 to $125,000. Cost, of course, depends upon the size of your second home, location, demand and the availability of land. The cost of furnishing and equipping your place kicks the price up another ten percent or more. You'll have to solve the question of security and maintenance if it's not included. Unless you can pay cash for your year-round escape, the high interest rates will add significantly to the already high cost of purchase.

Certainly the second home is an attractive alternative for those who can afford it. Yet many well-to-do people have purchased interval ownership simply because it provides them with more positive answers to their biggest concern—the hassles of whole ownership. Instead of a large outlay of cash for a down payment on a second home, they'd just as soon use that same amount of money to own a few prime interval weeks in their favorite vacation area. And leave the maintenance and security in the manager's hands. And share the costs with their neighbors on a smaller scale, without all the hassles of having to open up or shut down their second home.

If you will eventually be using your second home for retirement, you will have gained the added advantage of permanent residence in a resort location. If you will use it only for vacations, you may be able to recapture some of your investment by renting your weeks, although you probably won't do much better than to break even.

CHAPTER 3

How to Buy Your Resort Timeshare

By now you have a reasonably good idea of what resort timesharing is all about. You like the idea of curbing the escalating costs of vacations, or perhaps you've been looking for a nice little place in which to make a moderate investment. With resort timesharing becoming so popular, the number of areas and resorts from which to choose is practically limitless. So before you buy, consider these suggestions to make sure that you'll be happy with your final selection.

While exotic vacation spots like Hawaii, Las Vegas and Florida seem to have hundreds of attractive resorts, developments in little-publicized areas often offer one-of-a-kind vacations that could be just right for you. So weigh the pros and cons; consider your needs and what the various resorts have to offer. You will probably be delighted with your decision.

KNOW YOUR VACATION HABITS

If you've vacationed before, it's a simple matter to discuss with your family what you agree constitutes a good time and good value. You may want to make a few notes. Here are some questions to consider:

1. How often do you vacation—more than once a year, once a year, occasionally, or seldom?

   If you take frequent, annual or even occasional vacations, you should look into timesharing.

2. Do you like to vacation in one place, a few places, or a great variety of places?

   The answer will guide you toward the type of resort offering that is best for you. It may indicate that you should choose a good-quality resort and time period because you'll utilize the exchange program frequently. Gather information on what interval resorts exist in your favorite resort areas; writing to the chamber of commerce or a major real estate broker in the area can provide you with a wealth of preliminary information on what is available and the types of programs offered.

3. What do you like to do on vacation?

   Skiing or golf or tennis may rank as the prime recreational activity in your family; make up a list of what you must have on vacation to make it fun, as well as other interests such as night life, shopping and sightseeing. Now look for a resort that offers these activities.

4. How will you travel to a resort?

   Knowing how far you are willing to travel and how much you can spend on transportation will have a bearing upon where you select your resort. Don't forget that the exchange program offers exciting alternatives if you think you will occasionally be able to afford a longer trip.

5. How many people will be with you?

   This can be a tough question; parents may have teenage children who will move out in a few years, only to return as a visiting new family to share vacation togetherness. If you are vacationing with children, transportation cost plays an important role in resort selection; you should also bear in mind how many visitors—family and friends—you may have when you plan sleeping accommodations.

6. When do you vacation and for how many weeks?

   If your annual vacation is for more than one week, think back on how much of your time was spent away from home, and at what time of the year, in order to select the season and number of weeks best suited to you. If you vacation for two or more consecutive weeks, you'll be in the majority, and a purchase of consecutive weeks is a real plus should you want to rent or sell them later.

7. How much do you spend for a week's accommodations?

   Your pattern for the past few years may have been one of increasing quality and cost—or the higher cost may simply be the result of inflation. The frequency and expense of your vacations will be an important consideration in determining what to spend for your interval purchase. A rule of thumb: interval vacations are cost efficient if your purchase can reach a break-even point anywhere from eight to 15 years when compared with the total amount of money you'd spend on rent in that time. Inflation factors should also be taken into account.

8. What kind of people do you like to have around you?

   If you often plan vacations with friends, will they be interested in being neighbors, buying jointly with you in the same unit? Or is your immediate family your only concern? If you would like to make new friends, interval vacations put you into contact with other families who are on the same schedule at your resort year after year. One nice feature of timesharing is that you're usually among people with similar interests.

9. What are your vacation goals?

Will you be able to commit yourself to the same time period every year? Are comfort and convenience important objectives? Do you prefer structured advance planning and assured reservations, or will you opt to take chances on accommodations in order to retain last-minute flexibility?

Go over your list carefully and sort out your priorities, and you can then be pretty confident about what to look for in resort selection.

KNOW YOUR ECONOMIC LIMITATIONS

Once you've accepted the concept and found the resort you want, you'll have to consider your financial limitations. Since the average unit price is $6,000 and your plans call for two weeks of vacation every year, you're suddenly faced with a $12,000 decision, a little more than the price of a new car today. As with many consumer purchases, your interval weeks can be financed after the usual down payment.

If your income is sufficient or if you have ready cash, you've only to decide on whether to pay cash or finance your purchase. But if your budget is tight, you have to take a hard look at what you can afford. Be honest with yourself. You know your present situation and can estimate future income potential. You've established your vacation objectives and know that though annual vacation rentals may seem easier to live with because you just pay your bill when you leave the motel, you like the savings, lifestyle and long-term elements of interval vacations.

Beware. Here is where you may make your first mistake. You'll be tempted to buy two of the lowest-priced weeks simply because of economic factors. On paper, you'll be within your budget, and the salesperson may go along with your selection because your mind seems to be made up and he doesn't want to lose a sale. Your rationale will probably be that the price is right and the exchange network can come to your rescue in swapping for a more desirable location elsewhere. We'll cover the problems that may arise from putting too much emphasis on the exchange later; for now, the point is: buy just what you need. If the two lower-priced weeks really meet your needs, then by all means take them. But if you're buying in a time period that is not compatible with your usual vacation period, you may not be able to use your weeks often enough to enjoy the savings they were intended to provide. Make your decision on the basis that you're going to use those weeks for your next vacation and for many years to come. If that means you have to buy more expensive weeks in order to fit them into your vacation schedule, do it. Have the salesperson work out the figures after deducting your down payment. If you can live with the monthly payments, welcome to the wonderful world of resort timesharing. If you can't live with those costs, you may want to cut back on the number of weeks you are buying.

Sometimes a buyer selects too many weeks and ends up cancelling his entire interval package after he gets home and decides he can't afford it. Most states have laws to protect you in these cases, because you have a "cooling off" period of from three to 15 days and can receive 100 percent refund of all monies paid should you decide to cancel. (We'll cover your buying rights in more detail in Chapter 9.) But if you truly like the resort and the values offered, don't panic and miss out on that part of the package that you will enjoy and can afford. You can simply tell the resort owner that you've got to cut back to the two weeks that really meet your needs. Most developers will be happy to oblige—they would prefer to have satisfied buyers who will refer their friends and associates to the resort as future customers. Just remember that this is a significant purchase, and you should exercise some caution. If the resort is a good one, the developer will find buyers for his low-cost weeks just as he will for his more expensive weeks.

The resort's rate of sales and stage of sellout may have some bearing upon your decisions. If you're considering buying an extra week in a resort that is in its early stages, you may want to forego the added week until you give more thought to your finances. If the resort is nearing sellout, you may choose to buy the extra week simply because soon it may not be available. If you vacation during the first three weeks of July, for example, there may only be a few units left for sale during those time periods. Once the developer sells those weeks, your only way of acquiring them is via a purchase from the new owner, should he wish to sell, or through a cancellation that puts the weeks back into the developer's hands. A good salesperson will keep you in mind should the latter happen, and give you right of first refusal.

WHAT TO LOOK FOR IN A RESORT

Location Real estate experts say that there are only three prime elements in selecting property: location—location—location! For you, location merits two important considerations. Is the location area favorable to your personal tastes, and is the location of the resort in that area a good one?

Chances are you will be spending some time and money getting to your vacation area. If it's not near an airport, you'll have to drive, and so will other families who may wish to rent, buy or exchange for your resort at some future time. Value protection in your purchase will rely a great deal upon accessibility—how easily can anyone get there?

After accessibility, the location of the resort becomes important. There is a big difference in being right on the beach as opposed to being a mile away; of being near a ski slope versus having to travel another 50 miles to enjoy your favorite sport. Good access, when combined with good location, adds up to good timesharing.

Everyone likes to enjoy a bargain, and today's prices can be a steal if the resort is one of the best in a highly popular vacation area; growing popularity will create a very favorable supply-and-demand position for those with "supply" when inflation raises motel prices and tourists "demand" good accommodations. And you won't be faced with the prices and aggravations renters face when trying to find adequate accommodations in a tight-supply-and-high-demand area. While you may decide not to participate in resales or rentals, it's always good to know those options are available.

The Fun Package Vacations are more than lying on the beach or slaloming down a ski hill. Be sure that the surrounding area, as well as the resort, has an adequate mix of things you like to do to make your vacation a memorable one. Whether it's the natural environment, nearby shopping or night life, you should be happy enough with the activities offered to want to return annually.

In most cases, you're going to spend as much or more time outside as you will inside your unit. The majority of resorts, especially those built expressly for interval resort sharing, select locations close to plenty of recreational facilities.

Most resorts feature a large heated pool, barbecue grills, picnic areas. Many beach resorts will include sailboats, bicycles, shuffleboard, whirlpool bath, games, books and perhaps tennis right on the property. Resorts which feature skiing in winter months will have fireplaces and other indoor amenities to offset the cold weather outdoors, along with the usual warm-weather facilities for summer.

The Resort Ambiance Your participation in resort sharing should get you out of the motel mediocrity rut. The
concept is designed to provide a luxurious resort within
the average family's budget.

Vacations are special times and they should begin with
superior accommodations. Look for furnishings above
motel quality—they may even surpass what you enjoy at
home. The decor and appointments should make you feel
proud to have friends over, or give you the feeling that
you've stepped up in the world.

If you have a family, a kitchen/dining area is essential,
because restaurant breakfasts and lunches can quickly
run up your expenses. Most resorts have a washer-dryer
in the unit or a laundry room, so that you can do laundry,
if necessary, while on vacation, or pack up clean clothes
for your trip home, without the hassle of lugging clothes
to the laundromat.

Check the dishware and towels. You'll have an idea of
the developer's interest in quality via these minor—yet
revealing—items; if they're what you'd expect in a second-rate motel, beware. The resort may skimp in more
important areas as well.

There is no reason for poor-quality materials or shoddy
furnishings in an interval unit. Just as your vacation savings will come from sharing the cost with others, the first-
quality products in the apartment won't cost that much
more for the developer, nor for the eventual replacement
when shared among the buyers.

The Resort Management The success of any business
depends on the people involved. How well is the product
serviced after it is sold? You may recall a favorite motel
in which, despite many shortcomings, you have had
memorable vacations simply because the management
was concerned about your well-being from the moment
you arrived to the time you left. Or you may have paid an
outrageous daily rate at a swank hotel with all the trim-
mings and wound up being monumentally disappointed
because the service was appalling.

Resorts are people-sensitive businesses that will be as superior or as mediocre as the staff makes them. Interval resorts are no exception. The key is having a management operation that understands that different families will move into the units every week of the year and believes that the new occupants shouldn't have to care what took place before their arrival—they just want to enjoy their vacations.

Because interval vacationers "belong" and will be repeat visitors year after year, the management company must meet an important challenge. The "members of the club" expect a certain level of service not only during their vacations, but to protect the value of their investments over the years. And it is common sense for the developer, especially if he is to reclaim control after expiration of a right-to-use offer, to want his investment maintained at "like-new" levels.

Regardless of the type of interval program you buy, you will be required to pay a management fee. The budgets are designed to provide for *good* management. If management falls below acceptable levels, speak up.

Review closely any resort that has an inordinately long contract with the management company, unless the resort is of the right-to-use form and the management is strongly controlled by the resort owner or developer. A five- or ten-year contract is called a "grandfather" agreement, and in interval ownership it can hinder severely the control needed by the owners' association over management performance. An initial contract of two or three years with annual or two-year renewals will keep the management company on its toes. A shorter contract will also allow the association to make the adjustments necessary for improved service or to increase the budget. The contract will also have some provisions for termination should standards fall below specified levels.

If your resort reverts back to the owner or developer some time in the future, he'll retain ultimate control over management because after your agreement expires, the resort is again his exclusive property. Therefore, his interest in the long run is the same as yours—to set and maintain high standards.

The Developer Developing resort sharing properties is a tough business, and not every developer has the flair and the financial backing to build or convert a complex into a first-rate timesharing property. A failing motel operator who thinks his salvation lies in converting to an interval resort may commit the same mistakes he made in running his motel.

It is important that the developer provide you with sufficient evidence that he has the means of delivering to you the vacation home he promises. Whether you buy a unit under construction or one being converted from another use, the developer will need sufficient cash flow to cover that critical time between initial sales and completed construction.

Fortunately, the industry is attracting better-established developers than it could during the pioneering days of the concept. Whatever resorts you review, be sure to ask about the developer's achievements in the industry. If the resort is complete, it will provide enough evidence of his capabilities. If he finances customer purchases, the credibility of his bank may give a hint as to his financial standing.

A reputable developer will not hesitate to provide information about his company, its ideals and long-range management plans. If you're on vacation in his area, stop by the chamber of commerce for information, or chat with local merchants who know his work. You can check to see whether the developer is a member in good standing of the National Timesharing Council of the American Land Development Association. While membership doesn't guarantee a good reputation or vouch for the quality of the resort, its members are pledged to a strict code of ethics, and most of the top-notch companies belong or have applied for membership.

The Exchange Network Besides the advantages that come from a resort's affiliation with one of the exchange networks, membership also means that the resort and the developer have passed a stringent inspection. This does not guarantee that changes won't occur, but it does indicate that certain standards were met at the outset. If a resort doesn't belong to a network or hasn't yet received an answer to its application, wait until you know its final status before making your commitment.

The Vacation Calendar Not all resorts organize their weekly segments in the same manner, nor are they all based on a seven-night week. The most popular system utilizes a seven-day and seven-night week that begins and ends on Saturday, rather than one that has a Friday check-in and a Thursday check-out. As in a hotel, six hours is considered enough time between occupants for the maid service to clean the unit thoroughly; 24 hours is excessive and cuts into the vacationer's recreation time unnecessarily. A system of check-out by 9 A.M. or 10 A.M. will be followed by a check-in at 3 P.M. or 4 P.M.

The Saturday system helps avoid some of the hassles associated with weekend travel. Airports and roads are always busiest on Fridays and Sundays, while Saturday travel is less hectic for the whole family.

The calendar on pages 56 and 57 shows a typical annual vacation calendar that divides the year into its 52 segments, beginning with the first Saturday in January. While the dates may change by a day each year, the weeks remain similarly positioned so that week #1 falls after New Year's Day and week #52 before that holiday.

This calendar will be important for you, since you'll have to match your vacation schedule to the appropriately numbered weeks for translation onto your purchase agreement. (You may find yourself using a new jargon—"intervalese"—with statements like "I'd like to trade a week #5 for a week #10" or "What are my advantages in

INTERVAL RESORT SHARING CALENDAR

Week #	1982	1983	1984	Week #	1982	1983	1984
1	Jan. 2 - 9	Jan. 1 - 8	Jan. 7 - 14	27	July 3 - 10	July 2 - 9	7 - 14
2	9 - 16	8 - 15	14 - 21	28	10 - 17	9 - 16	14 - 21
3	16 - 23	15 - 22	21 - 28	29	17 - 24	16 - 23	21 - 28
4	23 - 30	22 - 29	28 - 4	30	24 - 31	23 - 30	28 - 4
5	30 - 6	29 - 5	Feb. 4 - 11	31	31 - 7	30 - 6	Aug. 4 - 11
6	Feb. 6 - 13	Feb. 5 - 12	11 - 18	32	Aug. 7 - 14	Aug. 6 - 13	11 - 18
7	13 - 20	12 - 19	18 - 25	33	14 - 21	13 - 20	18 - 25
8	20 - 27	19 - 26	25 - 3	34	21 - 28	20 - 27	25 - 1
9	27 - 6	26 - 5	Mar. 3 - 10	35	28 - 4	27 - 3	Sept. 1 - 8
10	Mar. 6 - 13	Mar. 5 - 12	10 - 17	36	Sept. 4 - 11	Sept. 3 - 10	8 - 15
11	13 - 20	12 - 19	17 - 24	37	11 - 18	10 - 17	15 - 22
12	20 - 27	19 - 26	24 - 31	38	18 - 25	17 - 24	22 - 29
13	27 - 3	26 - 2	Apr. 31 - 7	39	25 - 2	24 - 1	Oct. 29 - 6
14	Apr. 3 - 10	Apr. 2 - 9	7 - 14	40	Oct. 2 - 9	Oct. 1 - 8	6 - 13
15	10 - 17	9 - 16	14 - 21	41	9 - 16	8 - 15	13 - 20
16	17 - 24	16 - 23	21 - 28	42	16 - 23	15 - 22	20 - 27
17	24 - 1	23 - 30	May 28 - 5	43	23 - 30	22 - 29	27 - 3
18	May 1 - 8	May 30 - 7	5 - 12	44	30 - 6	29 - 5	Nov. 3 - 10
19	8 - 15	7 - 14	12 - 19	45	Nov. 6 - 13	Nov. 5 - 12	10 - 17
20	15 - 22	14 - 21	19 - 26	46	13 - 20	12 - 19	17 - 24
21	22 - 29	21 - 28	26 - 2	47	20 - 27	19 - 26	24 - 1
22	29 - 5	28 - 4	June 2 - 9	48	27 - 4	26 - 3	Dec. 1 - 8
23	June 5 - 12	June 4 - 11	9 - 16	49	Dec. 4 - 11	Dec. 3 - 10	8 - 15
24	12 - 19	11 - 18	16 - 23	50	11 - 18	10 - 17	15 - 22
25	19 - 26	18 - 25	23 - 30	51	18 - 25	17 - 24	22 - 29
26	26 - 3	25 - 2	July 30 - 7	52	25 - 1	24 - 31	29 - 5

owning a week #6 for skiing and a week #43 for the fall foliage season?")

Because of the changing of dates from year to year, you may want to buy two consecutive weeks to cover a specific holiday you want as part of your vacation program. Independence Day in the U.S. falls in week #26 in 1984 and in week #27 in 1982 and 1983. Easter will vary not only by the week over a period of years but will also change months from March to April.

Over seven years the resort calendar winds up with an extra week at the start of a year under this Saturday schedule (see 1983 versus 1984); this week can be used for extra maintenance, or it can be rented or split between the two adjacent occupants that year. In ownership resorts, the owners' association may rent out the extra week and apply the income to the operating budget.

INTERVAL VACATION CALENDAR
SATURDAY — SATURDAY

Week #	1981	1982	1983	1984	1985	1986	1987	1988
1	Jan. 3 - 10	Jan. 2 - 9	Jan. 1 - 8	Jan. 7 - 14	Jan. 5 - 12	Jan. 4 - 11	Jan. 3 - 10	Jan. 2 - 9
2	10 - 17	9 - 16	8 - 15	14 - 21	12 - 19	11 - 18	10 - 17	9 - 16
3	17 - 24	16 - 23	15 - 22	21 - 28	19 - 26	18 - 25	17 - 24	16 - 23
4	24 - 31	23 - 30	22 - 29	28 - 4	26 - 2	25 - 1	24 - 31	23 - 30
5	31 - 7	30 - 6	29 - 5	Feb. 4 - 11	Feb. 2 - 9	Feb. 1 - 8	31 - 7	30 - 6
6	Feb. 7 - 14	Feb. 6 - 13	Feb. 5 - 12	11 - 18	9 - 16	8 - 15	Feb. 7 - 14	Feb. 6 - 13
7	14 - 21	13 - 20	12 - 19	18 - 25	16 - 23	15 - 22	14 - 21	13 - 20
8	21 - 28	20 - 27	19 - 26	25 - 3	23 - 2	22 - 1	21 - 28	20 - 27
9	28 - 7	27 - 6	26 - 5	Mar. 3 - 10	Mar. 2 - 9	Mar. 1 - 8	28 - 7	27 - 5
10	Mar. 7 - 14	Mar. 6 - 13	Mar. 5 - 12	10 - 17	9 - 16	8 - 15	Mar. 7 - 14	Mar. 5 - 12
11	14 - 21	13 - 20	12 - 19	17 - 24	16 - 23	15 - 22	14 - 21	12 - 19
12	21 - 28	20 - 27	19 - 26	24 - 31	23 - 30	22 - 29	21 - 28	19 - 26
13	28 - 4	27 - 3	26 - 2	Apr. 31 - 7	Apr. 30 - 6	Apr. 29 - 5	28 - 4	26 - 2
14	Apr. 4 - 11	Apr. 3 - 10	Apr. 2 - 9	7 - 14	6 - 13	5 - 12	Apr. 4 - 11	Apr. 2 - 9
15	11 - 18	10 - 17	9 - 16	14 - 21	13 - 20	12 - 19	11 - 18	9 - 16
16	18 - 25	17 - 24	16 - 23	21 - 28	20 - 27	19 - 26	18 - 25	16 - 23
17	25 - 2	24 - 1	23 - 30	May 28 - 5	May 27 - 4	26 - 3	25 - 2	23 - 30
18	May 2 - 9	May 1 - 8	May 30 - 7	5 - 12	4 - 11	May 3 - 10	May 2 - 9	May 30 - 7
19	9 - 16	8 - 15	7 - 14	12 - 19	11 - 18	10 - 17	9 - 16	7 - 14
20	16 - 23	15 - 22	14 - 21	19 - 26	18 - 25	17 - 24	16 - 23	14 - 21
21	23 - 30	22 - 29	21 - 28	26 - 2	25 - 1	24 - 31	23 - 30	21 - 28
22	30 - 6	29 - 5	28 - 4	June 2 - 9	June 1 - 8	June 31 - 7	30 - 6	28 - 4
23	June 6 - 13	June 5 - 12	June 4 - 11	9 - 16	8 - 15	7 - 14	June 6 - 13	June 4 - 11
24	13 - 20	12 - 19	11 - 18	16 - 23	15 - 22	14 - 21	13 - 20	11 - 18
25	20 - 27	19 - 26	18 - 25	23 - 30	22 - 29	21 - 28	20 - 27	18 - 25
26	27 - 4	26 - 3	25 - 2	July 30 - 7	July 29 - 6	July 28 - 5	27 - 4	25 - 2
27	July 4 - 11	July 3 - 10	July 2 - 9	7 - 14	6 - 13	5 - 12	July 4 - 11	July 2 - 9
28	11 - 18	10 - 17	9 - 16	14 - 21	13 - 20	12 - 19	11 - 18	9 - 16
29	18 - 25	17 - 24	16 - 23	21 - 28	20 - 27	19 - 26	18 - 25	16 - 23
30	25 - 1	24 - 31	23 - 30	28 - 4	27 - 3	26 - 2	25 - 1	23 - 30
31	Aug. 1 - 8	31 - 7	30 - 6	Aug. 4 - 11	Aug. 3 - 10	Aug. 2 - 9	Aug. 1 - 8	Aug. 30 - 6
32	8 - 15	Aug. 7 - 14	Aug. 6 - 13	11 - 18	10 - 17	9 - 16	8 - 15	6 - 13
33	15 - 22	14 - 21	13 - 20	18 - 25	17 - 24	16 - 23	15 - 22	13 - 20
34	22 - 29	21 - 28	20 - 27	25 - 1	24 - 31	23 - 30	22 - 29	20 - 27
35	29 - 5	28 - 4	27 - 3	Sept. 1 - 8	Sept. 31 - 7	Sept. 30 - 6	29 - 5	27 - 3
36	Sept. 5 - 12	Sept. 4 - 11	Sept. 3 - 10	8 - 15	7 - 14	6 - 13	Sept. 5 - 12	Sept. 3 - 10
37	12 - 19	11 - 18	10 - 17	15 - 22	14 - 21	13 - 20	12 - 19	10 - 17
38	19 - 26	18 - 25	17 - 24	22 - 29	21 - 28	20 - 27	19 - 26	17 - 24
39	26 - 3	25 - 2	24 - 1	Oct. 29 - 6	Oct. 28 - 5	Oct. 27 - 4	26 - 3	24 - 1
40	Oct. 3 - 10	Oct. 2 - 9	Oct. 1 - 8	6 - 13	5 - 12	4 - 11	Oct. 3 - 10	Oct. 1 - 8
41	10 - 17	9 - 16	8 - 15	13 - 20	12 - 19	11 - 18	10 - 17	8 - 15
42	17 - 24	16 - 23	15 - 22	20 - 27	19 - 26	18 - 25	17 - 24	15 - 22
43	24 - 31	23 - 30	22 - 29	27 - 3	26 - 2	25 - 1	24 - 31	22 - 29
44	31 - 7	30 - 6	29 - 5	Nov. 3 - 10	Nov. 2 - 9	Nov. 1 - 8	31 - 7	29 - 5
45	Nov. 7 - 14	Nov. 6 - 13	Nov. 5 - 12	10 - 17	9 - 16	8 - 15	Nov. 7 - 14	Nov. 5 - 12
46	14 - 21	13 - 20	12 - 19	17 - 24	16 - 23	15 - 22	14 - 21	12 - 19
47	21 - 28	20 - 27	19 - 26	24 - 1	23 - 30	22 - 29	21 - 28	19 - 26
48	28 - 5	27 - 4	26 - 3	Dec. 1 - 8	Dec. 30 - 7	Dec. 29 - 6	28 - 5	26 - 3
49	Dec. 5 - 12	Dec. 4 - 11	Dec. 3 - 10	8 - 15	7 - 14	6 - 13	Dec. 5 - 12	Dec. 3 - 10
50	12 - 19	11 - 18	10 - 17	15 - 22	14 - 21	13 - 20	12 - 19	10 - 17
51	19 - 26	18 - 25	17 - 24	22 - 29	21 - 28	20 - 27	19 - 26	17 - 24
52	26 - 2	25 - 1	24 - 31	29 - 5	28 - 4	27 - 3	26 - 2	24 - 31

Maintenance Cost and Coverage Because the unit you are buying will be in constant use and must withstand years of continued occupancy, it is essential that your resort provide top-notch maintenance to keep the unit "like new" during your contract period. While general cleaning and light maintenance can be done on a weekly basis, at least one week annually should be set aside for major repairs, overhaul and possible replacement of furnishings and equipment.

The annual maintenance week is usually planned for some time during the slower season of the year. Refurbishing could cover everything from shampooing the carpets, cleaning draperies and painting to replacing kitchen appliances and furniture.

Questions to ask include: "Is there a full-time maintenance man on the job?" "Whom will I call for emergencies?" "What are the allowances for normal wear and tear before breakage is charged to occupants?" "What is the availability of the local labor market?" "Will inflation have an unusually high effect on maintenance budgets in future years?" "What does the maintenance budget cover, and is it adequate?" "What doesn't it cover?"

One area of timesharing that is not automatically protected from inflation is maintenance. A well-conceived budget should allow for the normal cost-of-living increases, but under good supervision it can allow for important anti-inflation measures to protect owners from drastic increases.

A skimpy budget may have been designed as a come-on for buyers or may simply be the result of poor planning. A budget that seems very high may be more realistic than you'd like to admit, or it, too, could be miscalculation. While it will be difficult for you to assess what a reasonable maintenance fee should be, a check with comparable resorts or condominiums in the area will give you an idea. If you find great discrepancies, ask your resort management about it and, if you don't get straightforward answers, think twice about that resort.

In attempting to keep maintenance fees sensible, some resorts set two separate fees; one will cover the normal costs regardless of occupancy and the other, a per diem fee, will include additional utility and cleaning costs. The per diem charges do not apply if the apartment is vacant during your time slot. If you rent or loan your unit, you'll be charged the per diem; you'll want to take this into consideration when budgeting for rental rates or use by friends.

The staggering of maintenance weeks can be important. Some resorts simply plan to close all units for the same week each year. This may be practical for a small resort but not for a large one; there will be problems finding a large enough crew, and dozens of units cannot be efficiently serviced within seven days. Staggered weeks allow an experienced crew enough time to move through the resort in phases and do a thorough job.

Taxes Taxes are, of course, subject to inflation. They will either be a part of your fees or billed separately. Rates are established by the county tax assessor and the association may act as the central clearing house for the proportionate distribution to each owner on a unit basis. Keep in mind that increases are shared by all owners and, thus, each unit incurs only a small increase. Real estate taxes are deductible when filing income taxes, and you may want to ask about separate billing. Developers selling right-to-use types of interval generally don't give you a tax breakdown, because the taxes cover all the developer's property and he will simply estimate what your share will be for the term of your contract and include it as a flat fee in maintenance charges. You can ask him for a breakdown, of course, but the cost of the paperwork involved probably wouldn't be worth the very few dollars you'd be able to deduct in the end.

Occupancy Limits Make sure you understand the occupancy limitations of your unit, not only for your own requirements but as an indication of how much wear and tear the unit will receive. If there are no limits, beware! Overcrowding means faster deterioration, more frequent replacement of equipment and additional maintenance —for a considerable increase in your annual fees.

Most resorts restrict or ban animals from the premises. While you may have a close attachment to your cat or dog, pets can create undue wear and tear on carpets and furniture, and they can be noisy. Some people welcome this restriction as an opportunity to take a guilt-free vacation from their pet. Your resort may be able to assist in locating a good kennel nearby, if you can't leave your animal at home.

Remember that the rules and regulations have been designed to protect the majority of vacationers, not to place unnecessary obstructions in your way. Management simply has to be able to assure the best vacation possible for all concerned.

The Price This will probably be the most important consideration once you have decided to buy into a timesharing resort. Here are a few guidelines concerning costs:

If the resort is in its early stages, special introductory prices may be in effect to reward early buyers. Most developers follow the condominium concept of graduating prices according to completion stages. This does not mean that buying later will result in a penalty, since the sale price will still be good value at the time of completion. It simply gives early participants some compensation for having to wait longer for occupancy.

To establish whether the resort you like offers good value for the money, compare it to others on the market, and look into resale prices as well. The best idea is to simply compare the costs of renting and controlling an interval unit during the time your purchase will cover. If your cost to rent comparable lodging over ten years is $400 per week, or $4,000—without rental inflation— then your purchase of a $4,000 week will bring you to a break-even stage after ten years. Granted, these figures do not take into account maintenance fees, but rent inflation may be significantly more over the years than your maintenance costs for the same periods, and a more detailed analysis of rental inflations versus maintenance costs would make ownership even more attractive.

The longer the period of your interval contract, the smaller your weekly amortized cost for accommodations will become. A $6,000 interval package costs $300 per week for 20 years and $150 per week for 40 years. Similar rental accommodations may cost $400 per week now, adding up to $4,000 in ten years, $8,000 in 20 years, $12,000 in 30 years and $16,000 in 40 years—without any allowance for inflation. Savings to the interval owner are quite evident here.

This does not mean that shorter-term offerings are not good value. The developer's objective is to offer better quality at lower prices than rentals, and he can do so regardless of the contract period involved. A ten-year program of 100 percent occupancy even with lower weekly rates is as attractive to him as it is to you.

After you've determined the number of years it will take you to break even with renting, determine how many more years you have left on your purchase agreement. Other than the ongoing maintenance fees, the remaining years of vacation represent low-cost or free time. If your interval provides an equity basis or ownership interest in the resort for an indeterminable length of time (usually the life of the building), your contract may provide for 40 or more years of vacations at one set price. This property remains part of your estate, of course, for further enjoyment by your heirs. Or you may reach a point where you wish to rent or sell your unit week.

Remember, however, that your main objective in time-sharing is to have really wonderful vacations for as many years as you wish. If your unit also turns out to be a profitable investment, then so much the better. While real estate is generally considered to be a good investment, your developer can't offer you any guarantees.

RESORT TIMESHARING

THEORETICAL COMPARISON FIGURES FOR 20 YEARS' RENTING VS. INTERVAL RESORT SHARING AT APPROXIMATELY 10% INFLATION PER YEAR

Renting Your Vacations

Year	Daily Accommodations Cost*	Cost Per 7-Day Vacation	Cumulative Cost by Year
1980	$ 88	$ 616	$ 616
1981	96	672	1,288
1982	105	735	2,023
1983	115	805	2,828
1984	126	882	3,710
1985	138	966	4,676
1986	151	1,057	5,733
1987	166	1,162	6,895
1988	182	1,274	8,169
1989	200	1,400	9,569
1990	220	1,540	11,109
1991	242	1,694	12,803
1992	266	1,862	14,665
1993	292	2,044	16,709
1994	321	2,247	18,956
1995	353	2,471	21,427
1996	388	2,716	24,143
1997	426	2,982	27,125
1998	468	3,276	30,401
1999	514	3,598	33,999
			$33,999

* areas affected by 10% annual inflation
NOTE: Comparison illustrated is based on occupancy for 4 persons on a $6,000 cash purchase for the average interval week. The comparison would differ on a financed interval purchase depending upon the down payment, amount financed, interest rate and payments as affected by the number of years on the mortgage. All figures have been rounded to the nearest dollar for the sake of simplicity.

High prices for interval units won't necessarily indicate high developer profits and lower values any more than low prices signal a bargain too good to pass up. A developer bases his prices on seasonal demands, with a goal of attaining a reasonable profit for the 51 weeks he's selling in each unit. As in any vacation arrangement,

Year	Daily Apartment Cost	Amortized Cost per Week	$183 Maintenance*	Cumulative Cost by Year
		$6,000 Interval Resort Program (Cash Purchase)		
1980	$ 69	$ 300	$ 183	$ 483
1981	72	300	201	984
1982	74	300	221	1,505
1983	78	300	243	2,048
1984	81	300	267	2,615
1985	85	300	293	3,208
1986	89	300	322	3,830
1987	94	300	354	4,484
1988	99	300	389	5,173
1989	105	300	427	5,900
1990	111	300	469	6,669
1991	117	300	515	7,484
1992	125	300	566	8,350
1993	133	300	622	9,272
1994	142	300	684	10,256
1995	152	300	752	11,308
1996	163	300	827	12,435
1997	175	300	909	13,644
1998	188	300	999	14,943
1999	202	300	1,098	16,341
		$6,000	$10,341	$16,341

peak periods cost more and quiet seasons cost less. Your decision on what has good value for you should depend on a comparison between your vacation schedule in an interval unit and your rental alternatives.

Rental and Resales Services Sometime in the future you may plan not to use your unit and, rather than let your time that year expire, you may elect to rent it. You may have friends in mind who would enjoy your resort, or you may find a tenant yourself through a few well-placed ads. But if you don't want the hassle of finding a tenant and collecting the rent, you can have a local agent handle the whole transaction for a commission—usually in the 20 to 30 percent range, depending on the services he provides. (Agents occasionally pay for maid service for the week from their commission.) The developer will be able to suggest an agent.

If you eventually decide to resell your unit weeks, be sure that this is allowed under the terms of your purchase agreement. Many right-to-use plans do not allow resale at a profit, either because of local laws or as a deterrent to stimulating purchase merely for speculation. And because your purchase of right-to-use is not considered a real estate transaction, the salesman may not represent the purchase as an investment unless the resort is listed with the Securities and Exchange Commission. SEC registration is a long, involved and costly process, and sales personnel would be required to have securities licenses as well as real estate licenses (see pages 164–165 for more detail). The industry stance is that even though interval ownership is a transaction in real estate, sales people should also avoid presenting interval as an investment, since the SEC may become involved.

If you have the right to sell your unit weeks, you may also need some assistance through local brokers or sales agents. Because you may live a considerable distance from the resort, trying to sell it yourself could be time-consuming and difficult. You need an agent familiar with the resort who has experience in interval sales. The resort should be able to provide you with a few agents who already have listings and know how to handle the paperwork quickly and efficiently.

BENEFITS OF CASH AND FINANCE PURCHASING

If you've selected the vacation weeks that will be best for you and have the cash available, the best idea would be to sign your check and take pleasure in the fact that you've just purchased several years of vacations at the best terms possible. From an inflation standpoint, a cash purchase gives you the best bargaining position with the developer (if he can offer extra incentives for cash). It also shortens the time to break even, in comparison with accumulated rental costs, when interest costs are not added to your purchase price.

Your cash position may preclude paying outright, or you may wish to use your available cash as a downpayment on more weeks under a finance plan offered by the developer. In the days when interest rates were more reasonable, people preferred to leverage their buying power by using their cash only for down payments to control the greatest amount of property possible. When inflation was ten percent or less and ten-year bank rates were at ten percent interest, you could justify their approach to leveraging. While you ended up paying more for the property, inflation was hand-in-hand with interest rates and your property values would be worth that much more after ten years. In today's economy, when ten percent interest is no longer shocking but desirable, the leveraging approach is less attractive due to the high cost of financing. The inflation you're trying to beat has led to increasingly high interest rates, and you have no assurances that your extra weeks will be of proportionate value in the long run. Unless you know something special about the resort and the potential for making money on additional weeks beyond your personal vacation period, don't speculate. The history of owner sales is too recent to guarantee a good return on your investment.

The interest on financed payments is deductible on income tax returns, and some people will find that financed purchases put them in a better tax position. If you're in the 50 percent tax bracket, for example, you only pay the equivalent of about one-half of the interest since your tax deduction is paying the difference. Thus, even with interest rates as high as 20 percent, people in upper tax brackets end up with a realized interest of ten percent—just like "the good old days."

AN EXAMPLE OF A FINANCED SALE

The illustration on page 67 covers the basic arithmetic and payment obligations involved with an interest rate of 14.85 percent, in a financed sale consummated by an affiliated broker.

You'll note that the purchaser bought three weeks in January (weeks #2, #3 and #4) for $16,500, and received an inspection travel allowance of $600, for a net of $15,900. The resort required a 20 percent down payment, or $3,200 (figures are rounded out), plus closing and legal costs of approximately $330, to bring the purchaser's total cash outlay to roughly $3,500. Able to get ten-year financing at 14.85 percent, the buyer would make monthly payments of about $200 for the duration of the mortgage—or he could pay it off at any time.

This transmittal form is not the final sales agreement; the final one would be forthcoming from the resort's processing or sales office and reflect further details. The purchaser is financing a balance of $12,700 and the interest would be deductible on his income tax return to the tune of about $1,174.64 annually.

The finance or installment approach to buying vacation real estate follows the same processes as buying a home. The differences may be that either the developer or his bank may be the lender, and the terms offered seldom exceed ten years with the norm at five or seven years. You can choose to arrange your own financing and pay cash to the developer—some buyers can obtain lower interest rates elsewhere—or you may wish to consolidate your loan transactions at your present bank.

The shorter the finance period, the less interest you will pay. Buying a home over a long term may be necessary in order to make the monthly payments affordable, but it could also bring the cost of your home to double its original purchase price. Because of the much smaller amount involved in your interval purchase, you may find five or seven years more than adequate to budget an af-

Typical Transaction Transmittal Sheet

THIS AGREEMENT ALONG WITH PROPER REMITTANCE IS FOR THE PURPOSE OF RESERVING INTERVAL UNIT WEEKS AND PREPARING THE PURCHASE AGREEMENT AND ALL ACCOMPANYING PAPERS.

DATE __1 May 1981__ RESORT __Sand Castle Beach Club__

CLIENT:

HUSBAND'S NAME __John S. Smith__ SOCIAL SECURITY NO. __037-24-2983__

WIFE'S NAME __Mary D. Smith__ SOCIAL SECURITY NO. __038-24-2980__

STREET ADDRESS __6 French Street__

CITY __Providence__ STATE __R.I.__ ZIP __02915__

HOME PHONE (401) __437-1900__ BUSINESS PHONE (401) __437-1900__

TOTAL NUMBER OF FAMILY MEMBERS __4__ ADULTS __2__ CHILDREN __2__

UNIT	WEEKS	PRICE
215	2	$ 5,500
215	3	$ 5,500
215	4	$ 5,500
___	___	$ ___

TOTAL AMOUNT ... $ 16,500

LESS __Travel__ $ 600

LESS ___ $ ___

LESS ___ $ ___

NET PURCHASE PRICE $ 15,900

This section is (ESTIMATED) and exact figures are computed at closing with necessary adjustments made at that time.

*1. LEGAL AND TITLE .... $ 175.00 ⎫ 334.00
*2. OTHER CLOSING COST .... $ 159.00 ⎭

COMPLETE FOLLOWING INSTRUCTIONS IF FINANCING REQUESTED

3. NET PURCHASE PRICE .... $ 15,900
   15,900 x .20 = 3,180 to 3,200
4. LESS DOWN PAYMENT .... $ 3,200
5. AMOUNT FINANCED .... $ 12,700
6. TERMS __10__ YRS. (NO. OF PAYMENTS) ...... # 120
**7. ANNUAL PERCENTAGE RATE .... 14.85 %
**8. MONTHLY PAYMENT .... $ 203.72

*REFER TO RESORT FACT SHEET
**REFER TO ADD-ON MONTHLY PAYMENT CHART

AMOUNT DUE (CASH -- Net Purchase Price + Legal & Title + Closing Cost) .... $ 3,534.00
(FINANCE -- Downpayment + Legal & Title + Closing Cost)

Receipt is hereby acknowledged of initial amount of $ __500.00__ comprising part of AMOUNT DUE as set forth herein. Balance of $ __3,034.00__ is due on or before __15 June 1981__ .

In the event UNDERSIGNED does not complete purchase upon physical inspection said $ __500__ will be refunded promptly by the BROKER upon return of the UNDERSIGNED to their home.

☒ **Inspection Tour required**. Owners Information Report and Inspection Tour Agreement attached.

☐ **Inspection Tour not required**. Please prepare Purchase Agreement and return to CMSI broker affiliate.

CLIENT ACKNOWLEDGEMENT: _____ DATE __1 May 1981__
(Purchaser)

_____ DATE __1 May 1981__
(Purchaser)

CMSI BROKER AFFILIATE __John Doe__ PHONE (401) __437-1800__

SALES ASSOCIATE _____

RESORT — WHITE • CMSI — YELLOW COPY • BROKER — PINK COPY • CLIENT — GOLDENROD OSB-4 fordable monthly payment program without making the total cost prohibitive. The interest is tax deductible and financing may be your most comfortable solution. Whoever handles the financing, you'll want to check out any prepayment penalties should you elect to pay off your loan before its term of expiration.

In summary, use your good judgment on the answers you get to the 12 areas we have mentioned. Keep an open mind; the first resort you visit could be exactly right for you and you don't want to miss an opportunity because you're nervous about making a decision. The sales personnel will reflect the resort's operation; look for helpful assistance rather than a fast shuffle. The representative can easily present a strong case for his resort without high pressure if his approach is friendly and educational. If his sales pitch becomes heavy-handed, head for the door.

DOCUMENTS: HOW TO READ THE SMALL PRINT

If the resort you select offers right-to-use, the paperwork is fairly simple. There is no transfer of real estate or equity involved. You're dealing simply in a membership concept not unlike that of a country club or other retail sales transaction—with a few more details governing eligibility, rules and regulations. The contract specifies who/what/where/when/how and under what conditions you are entitled to occupy your unit weeks for the duration of your agreement.

The first page contains all the financial and membership details; the second or back page contains the small print detailing all the inclusions and restrictions. While the brochures may open your eyes to the comforts and activities that are part of your membership, it's this important document that deserves your careful attention. Read the small print; it only takes a few minutes and it isn't difficult to understand as long as you apply what you've learned to look for here.

Your documents *should* disclose to you any mortgages the resort or developer has on the property, and don't panic if you do encounter this information. Most resorts are bought or built with funds borrowed from reputable institutions. Your only concern is what happens if there is a default and a repossession by the lender.

Your concern can be expressed in a few words: "Is there a nondisturbance clause in my agreement?" This clause, when included in your agreement, protects your rights to use the resort accommodations and facilities without exception or interruption by the mortgage holder should the developer default on his mortgage. If the developer has a mortgage and does not have the mortgagor's assurance for nondisturbance written into your agreement, your vacation rights can be terminated at the discretion of the mortgagor should the developer default. The absence of this clause may indicate that the financial strength of the developer did not warrant that risk by the mortgagor; the amount remaining on the mortgage may require the lender to resell the whole resort, and any contracts for long-term occupancy are not of particular interest to the mortgagor, because they are not capable of producing further income. You've paid your money, yet you could face the prospect of either paying again or being deprived, under law, of further access to the resort. If you borrowed money to buy, you'll still be obligated to repay it; you'll have nothing to show for it if the lender chooses to terminate the interval program.

Since security is one of your goals, give a resort like this no more than a passing glance. Why take the risk? The lender just might repossess the resort and fulfill all the interval obligations—and he may be a better manager than the person you now have, but he might also decide that selling the units as $150,000 condominiums is the best way to recoup his loss. In that case, you will have no legal claim for any payments made under previous agreements, and your contract will have become null and void without the nondisturbance clause.

Again, there is nothing uncommon about finding a disclosure about a mortgage on the property; probably 80 percent of real estate in America is sold with a mortgage. Your concern is to have that nondisturbance clause in your contract on a right-to-use. Don't be without it.

If your resort features interval ownership, the paperwork is as lengthy and detailed as it is for buying a home or condominium. You are taking title or an equity interest in real estate property. Under the plan where ownership specifically designates your unit and weeks involved on a deed, your rights of nondisturbance have already been implemented legally and may not be altered.

Some potential buyers have difficulty with the idea of buying a piece of time in combination with real estate ownership. They understand how companies can buy an expensive computer under joint ownership and share its use, but real estate seems to have a mystique about it that shuns comparison.

This shouldn't be. The mystique about exactly what you own under interval ownership can be cleared up by reading the legal documents that accompany every ownership sale and are part of the presentation. You will have to wade through some legalese, but your agent or attorney can help you understand exactly how interval ownership works and explain how the law views your purchase.

While the following may seem a little tedious it is important that you understand all the points and mechanics of your ownership rights and obligations. (Some of these documents have been borrowed and adapted from regular condominium materials.)

The Declaration of Condominium (or "Condo Docs")

Most state laws require developers to file, record and distribute this declaration to all prospective buyers. It gives a complete description of the existing and proposed development covered under the sales agreement; it identifies the developer company and its executive officers and estimates the maintenance fees and insurance provisions for the property. It also defines operation and management responsibilities of the condominium association and the rules and regulations concerning occupancy of the units and use of the common facilities.

In essence, the declaration of condominium is a fact-filled booklet, complete with property plat maps (architecturally laid-out drawings showing all metes and boundaries), floor plans and all the legal coverage for the partitioning of ownership in the resort far beyond what you'll find in the brochures.

One of the items you may find if there is an existing mortgage on the property is a consent and joinder; this is an agreement verifying that the mortgage holder has joined in filing the declaration weeks to purchasers and that the developer has met his financial obligations to the mortgage holder. This agreement may not specify the amount of mortgage nor the terms, but these are not important omissions; your concern is only to get free and clear title to your share of the real estate that you bought. Naturally, your purchase is protected like any other real estate transaction—your monies are held in escrow for protection by a third party, either a financial institution or licensed escrow agent. Escrowed funds cannot be dispersed until the deed is recorded per your specifications, or, if you have changed your mind, until you request a full refund within the rescission (cooling-off) period. In lay terms, this means no one may have access to your dollars until the courthouse in your resort's county records your deed. If the resort has a mortgage, the developer is also required by the consent and joinder to file a partial release with the courthouse. This signifies that the developer has performed his financial obligation of directing necessary fund dispersion from the escrow account to the lawful recipients, and releases the developer from all obligations regarding your unit week with the mortgage holder.

If the resort is under construction, no escrow releases or recording of deeds can take place until a certificate of occupancy (CO) has been received from the local community verifying that the units in question are habitable in accord with applicable codes and standards. Some states permit developers to utilize escrow funds for construction and furnishings in order to accelerate issuance of the CO and resort completion.

I hope this information helps you understand the protective measures provided in real estate transactions. In ownership, the deed and escrow mechanics replace the nondisturbance clause used in right-to-use or membership resorts to protect the buyer. Interval ownership simply follows the accepted and proven guidelines for general real estate transactions. If you already own a home or condominium, you'll see the similarities instantly.

The Deed of Conveyance In case the purchase agreement doesn't explain interval ownership well enough, the deed received by every purchaser should clarify the terms (and a sample should be shown to you prior to purchase). It should read as follows:

> The Grantor . . . does hereby grant, bargain, sell and convey unto the aforesaid Grantee, their heirs, devisees, successors, and assigns, the following described property from 4:00 P.M. of the first day until 10:00 A.M. of the last day [whatever the detailed time period is] . . . during the below described unit week. . . .

This means that you have bought a week as described in the sales agreement and can do with it as you please. You may share your interest in the property with others (like a spouse) or pass it on to your children or anyone else in your will. Or, if you wish, you may rent or sell it like any other property.

The deed also clarifies the concept of "sharing" one unit with other weekly owners. The following clause will

ESTERO ISLAND BEACH CLUB

Deed of Conveyance

THIS DEED, *made this* _____ *day of* _____ *, 19* _____ *, by and between*
CAPTRAN DEVELOPMENT CORP., a Florida Corporation, as Grantor, Party of the First Part and _____
_____ *, as Grantee(s),*

whose Post Office address is: _____
Party(ies) of the Second Part.

WITNESSETH:

That the Grantor, in consideration of Ten Dollars and other good and valuable consideration to it paid by the Grantees, the receipt of which is hereby acknowledged, has bargained and sold, and by these presents does grant, bargain, sell and convey unto the aforesaid Grantees, their heirs, devisees, successors and assigns, the following described property from 12:00 noon of the first day until 12:00 noon on the last day assigned to said Grantees during the below described unit week(s) number(s) as said unit week(s) is numbered and defined in the Declaration of Condominium recorded in the public records of Lee County, Florida, in the Book and at the Page Number hereinafter described below, which estate is to be succeeded forthwith by a succession of other estates in consecutive and chronological order, revolving among the other unit weeks described in the aforesaid Declaration of Condominium, in order annually, it being the intent of this instrument that each unit week shall be considered a separate estate held separately and independently by the respective owners thereof for and during the period of time assigned to each in said Declaration of Condominium, each said estate being succeeded by the next in unending succession governed by said Declaration of Condominium until 12:00 noon on the first Saturday in 2021, at which date said estate shall terminate;

TOGETHER *with a remainder over in fee simple absolute, as tenant in common with the other owners of all the* unit weeks in the hereinafter described condominium parcel in that percentage interest determined and established by Exhibit Number 6 to the aforesaid Declaration of Condominium for the following described real estate located in the County of Lee and the State of Florida, as follows:

Unit Week(s) No(s). _____ , in Condominium Parcel _____

Unit Week(s) No(s). _____ , in Condominium Parcel _____

Unit Week(s) No(s). _____ , in Condominium Parcel _____

of Estero Island Beach Club, a Condominium, according to the Declaration of Condominium and exhibits thereof, as recorded in Official Records Book _____ at Page _____ in the Public Records of Lee County, Florida, all amendments thereto.

This conveyance is subject to and by accepting this Deed the Parties of the Second Part do hereby agree to assume the following:

1. Taxes for the current year and subsequent years;
2. Conditions, restrictions, limitations, reservations, easements, and other matters of record;
3. Declaration of Condominium of Estero Island Beach Club, a Condominium, and Exhibits attached thereto, and any amendments thereof.

The benefits and obligations hereunder shall inure to and be binding upon the heirs, executors, administrators, successors and assigns of the respective parties hereto. The Grantor does hereby fully warrant the title to such land, and will defend the same against the lawful claims of all persons whomsoever.

The plural number as used herein shall equally include the singular. The masculine or feminine gender as used herein shall equally include the neuter.

IN WITNESS WHEREOF, *Captran Development Corp., a Florida Corporation, has caused these* presents to be signed in name by its proper officer and its Corporate Seal to be affixed this _____ day of _____ , 19 _____

Signed, sealed and delivered in the presence of:

make you feel more secure as an owner concerned about your position with respect to other owners.

> . . . it being the intent of this instrument that each unit week shall be considered a separate estate held separately and independently by the respective owners thereof for and during the period of time assigned to each in said Declaration of Condominium. . . .

This clause specifically explains that your ownership of a unit week is held completely and separately from the people who own the week before or the week after you, or any other week, for that matter. If they default, your unit week is not affected and still belongs wholly and completely to you. By law your week is deemed completely unique and a separate piece of property.

The Purchase Agreement The front page of this document is similar to that used in a membership resort except for the reference to the transferral of real estate property; it spells out that both seller and buyer agree to the transaction regarding the unit weeks specified.

The second or back page differs greatly because of the transaction in real estate. Here, the details of the terms and conditions are spelled out in brief and easy-to-read paragraphs.

This instrument clearly defines each party's obligations and responsibilities in the transaction taking place; it even covers the possibilities of a discontinuance of the ownership offering (prior to closing) with full refund benefits to the buyer.

Again, if you've purchased a home or condominium, this document will hold little new except for the special circumstances surrounding interval ownership. A few minutes' review should cover the basics you need to know; if you encounter any confusing statements, don't hesitate to ask your resort representative to explain them in detail.

The Mortgage Deed This instrument is a familiar one to all who have purchased a home and assumed a mortgage. Under interval ownership usage, it specifies the indebtedness agreement between the buyer and the seller or the mortgagor, and the descriptions and usages of the property involved as recorded in the public records of the appropriate courthouse.

The mortgagor is required by law to send a notice of satisfaction to the courthouse upon fulfillment of the financial obligations; the deed and title to the units involved then become free and clear.

Title Insurance This document is issued to the buyer, at his option, as proof and protection that the deed he receives is valid and free from any defects. It's basically insurance against any future claims regarding free and clear title under the name of the buyer. Used only in the ownership form of interval resort sharing, the insurance coverage is in the amount of the purchase price and is a nominal one-time cost, usually to the buyer.

Other Documents Depending upon the geography and state laws, you may also be issued a number of other documents pertaining to flood hazard insurance or a separate prospectus as an overview of the resort and its offering. The number of documents neither guarantees nor diminishes the value of your purchase. All are either required by law for your protection or provided by the developer to further your understanding of the concept. So don't be intimidated by the paperwork. Developers want good standing within their community and state. By helping you with all the necessary forms, they show respect for you as a buyer, and they hope to send you back home to spread the good news about the terrific vacation opportunities and ethical businessmen at their resort.

Why All the Legalese? You may ask, "Why can't they write these legal documents in simple language?" It seems that attorneys write documents comprehensible only to other attorneys. Attempts are being made to simplify the language. However, the documents are written to comply with the prevailing expression of laws which originated from old English law precepts. For protection of all parties, the legalese is necessary to get the job done. The buyer isn't the only one who needs protection under law; sometimes it's the seller who can be victimized.

If you are unsure of any materials, contact your attorney for assistance. While he may not be familiar with the interval concept, he'll be knowledgeable enough in real estate matters to help you over the areas in question.

Water sports, tennis matches, golf and glamorous condominiums in a superb setting are featured at Sweetwater at Bear Lake, Utah.

The Estero Island Beach Club is an interesting example of an interval resort developed from an existing motel and reconstructed and refurbished into first-class accommodations.

The sun sets over the Gulf of Mexico at Estero Island Beach Club on Ft. Myers Beach, Florida.

The luxurious appointments in this living/dining room at Sanibel Beach Club II, Sanibel Island, Florida, allow vacationers to relax in comfort and style.

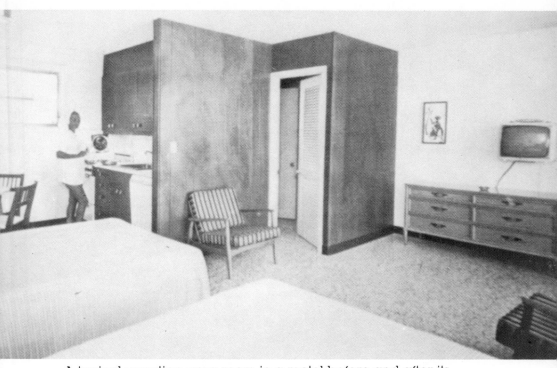

A typical vacation-area room in a motel before and after its conversion into a timesharing resort apartment.

One of the first resorts to be built expressly for interval owners, the Sanibel Beach Club in Florida was designed in cooperation with environmentalists.

An interior view at The Village at Palmetto Dunes, Hilton Head Island, South Carolina. Daily maid service is an option at most resorts.

Resort timesharing at the turn-of-the-century revival town of Park City, Utah, offers many extras for vacationers both summer and winter: powder skiing, championship golf, swimming, nightlife and dining.

San Francisco's prestigious Powell Place on famous Nob Hill, one of the newest developments in urban timesharing, where vacationers may enjoy all the delights of San Francisco and return to relax in their luxury suites.

The elegant entrance to Powell Place.

The Sweetwater at Waikiki, Hawaii, on the most famous beach on earth, provides the vacationer with all the amenities of a major resort.

Golfing at Kauai, Hawaii.

Vacationers at the Makaha Valley Plantation on the island of Oahu, Hawaii, may be found scuba diving, fishing or playing golf at nearby courses.

In a quiet Palm Springs, California, mountain cove, Sweetwater at
Indian Wells Racquet Club, cooled by date palms and private pools,
is a favorite golf resort.

Sunny Mallorca, the Balearic Islands, Spain, is the location for this Mediterranean Resort, which boasts a marina, horseback riding, golf and a wide variety of water sports.

Tucked into the Rocky Mountains, the Blue River Condominiums at Breckenridge, Colorado, are close to some of the finest skiing in the country, and offer outdoors enthusiasts fishing, horseback riding and hunting as well.

This inviting setting is part of the year-round resorts Residence Belle
Cote and Residence St. Jacques in Savoie, France, where
winter skiing is replaced in summer by tennis, swimming and
horseback riding.

Loch Rannoch Highland Lodges, set in the verdant Scottish highlands at Perthshire, is a year-round resort.

A view of San Carlos de Bariloche, Argentina, home of the oceanfront Bariloche Center resort. The exchange network allows you to exchange your vacation weeks for vacations in any affiliated resort around the world.

Villeneuve-Loubet on the French Riviera is the locale for Marina Bai des Anges, where guests play golf, enjoy water sports, and ski in the winter.

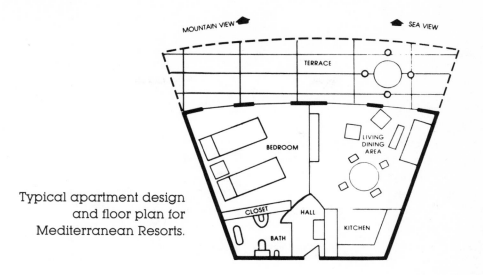

MOUNTAIN VIEW   SEA VIEW

TERRACE

BEDROOM

LIVING
DINING
AREA

CLOSET

HALL

KITCHEN

BATH

Typical apartment design
and floor plan for
Mediterranean Resorts.

Typical design and floor
plan for Mediterranean
Resorts.

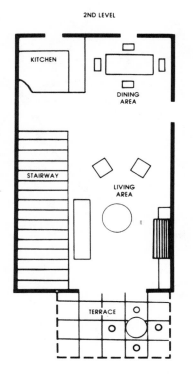

2ND LEVEL

KITCHEN

DINING
AREA

STAIRWAY

LIVING
AREA

TERRACE

MOUNTAIN VIEW   SEA VIEW

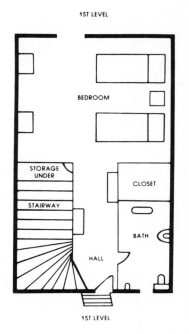

1ST LEVEL

BEDROOM

STORAGE
UNDER

CLOSET

STAIRWAY

BATH

HALL

1ST LEVEL

Efficiency, one- and two-
bedroom floor plans at the
Freeport Resort & Club
reflect design adaptation to
the circular buildings.

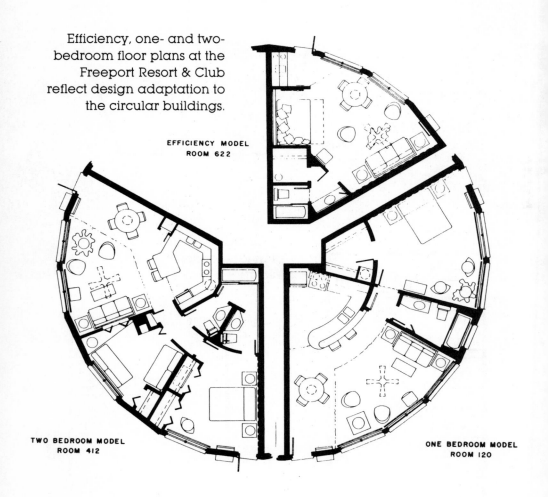

EFFICIENCY MODEL
ROOM 622

TWO BEDROOM MODEL
ROOM 412

ONE BEDROOM MODEL
ROOM 120

The Freeport Resort & Club on Grand Bahama Island. You can rent or
sell your timeshare unit at any time, or loan it to friends and relatives.

Parasailing is a growing sport at many timesharing resorts.

Located just 75 miles north of Vancouver, British Columbia, Canada, the Whistler Resort & Club offers six months of the Pacific Northwest's best skiing as well as winter and summer swimming. Sports enthusiasts can also enjoy excellent fishing, golf and mountain climbing.

One of the cozy interiors of the attractive Whistler Resort on Nita Lake
at the base of Whistler Mountain.

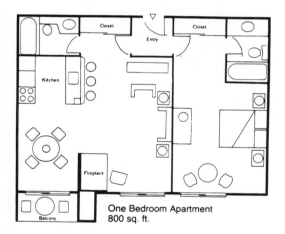

Whistler Resort & Club:
floor plans.

One Bedroom Apartment
800 sq. ft.

Two Bedroom Apartment
1088 sq. ft.

The interior of one of the apartments of the Caribbean Beach Club on Estero Island, Florida, where guests can sun and sail and get a taste of the Caribbean without leaving the United States.

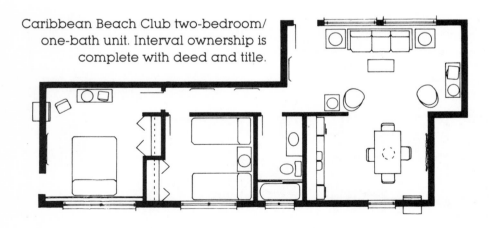

Caribbean Beach Club two-bedroom/ one-bath unit. Interval ownership is complete with deed and title.

The use of a sailboat at your front door is an added bonus for waterfront resort owners.

CHAPTER 4

What to Expect in Management and Maintenance

No matter where you live or what type of housing your family enjoys, you are responsible for some form of on-going management and maintenance. You know, from week to week, you will cut the lawn, wash the windows, fix the plumbing, vacuum the carpets, clean the bathrooms and so on. Think over the extra work you do when overnight guests come to visit in order to make their stay as comfortable as possible. Multiply this by several hundred, and you'll have an idea of what the management at an interval resort must plan for its "guests," and how much work is involved. As a prospective buyer in an interval resort, you'll want to know who the management company is and how you can be assured that they will keep your vacation home up to par year after year.

WHO IS THE MANAGEMENT COMPANY?

During the sales period, the developer or club offering the vacation program will be in charge, or will have delegated maintenance to a management company. A maintenance budget will have been established and the developer will stand behind that budget, usually for the duration of his involvement in sales and resort operations. Naturally, the resort and its apartments will be at their best as long as he has a vested interest in showing them properly to prospective buyers or members. Your objective is to have that quality maintained for the duration of your involvement.

If your resort ownership will eventually revert to the developer or the club, you'll not have any direct voice in who the management company will be. Since you have no real equity interest and your agreement only calls for the right to occupy accommodations, your interests will be superseded by those of the actual or eventual owner. Hopefully, that eventual owner will understand that it is in his best interest to maintain the property at peak condition.

Your right-to-use resort may well be a motel or hotel whose management has considerable experience in managing people and the daily logistics of the resort business. The only change could be in the weekly cost of rooms— your new position as a member may provide you with significant savings. Or you may be lucky enough to have a completely redecorated apartment, an appropriate maintenance budget and no sign of major problems with upkeep or replacement down the road.

You may not care about having a voice in the management, since none may really be needed; once you're satisfied that all the bases have been covered, your only concern is getting to the beach for the sunset or beating your neighbor at backgammon.

Not having a voice in management does not mean that no one will listen to your complaints about faulty operations. As the buyer, you purchased with the expectation of continued superior quality, and the management does have certain obligations to see that you are satisfied.

Since the management question involves much more individual participation under the interval ownership program, let us examine in greater detail the responsibilities and options for the owners.

Your ownership position at an interval resort carries with it the privilege and right to have a voice in the operation, as spelled out in your condominium documents. Essentially, an interval resort is structured along the same lines as a condominium with the only exception being the number of voices or votes that can have a bearing on operations. In a 40-unit interval resort, there will be 2,040 votes to be cast on any issue, if the resort sells 51 weeks. One vote is provided for each week owned, regardless of who owns it. Your presence will not be required for every vote—a proxy is standard and accepted procedure for absentee voting.

As an interval owner, you'll have a say in selecting the management company and the duration of its contract. Most resorts are turned over to the owners' association with a management operation already functioning, be it the one implemented by the developer or subsequently installed by the new board of directors of your association.

Board members do not fulfill management responsibilities; they oversee operations on your behalf as well as their own. The management can be a team hired individually by the board or an outside company of specialists. The initial budget provides for the fees and salaries of the staff needed to keep your resort running as if it were still a hotel or condominium. Maintenance and service is their function, and guidelines are established along with the budget. Unlike the management of a hotel, which reports to the owner and not the guests, interval management must answer to the owners as duly represented by the board of directors.

The board of directors is elected from within your group of interval owners for a period of one year. Most frequently, members live within close proximity to the resort or can travel to the resort often enough to effectively represent all the owners. Officers are elected from the board membership and are not paid for their work on your behalf, but they may receive budgeted expenses for costs incurred beyond the norm.

For all intents and purposes, your association is run like a business and established along the lines of any corporation. The board is responsible to the owners and the management is responsible to the board, although vacationing owners can work directly with the management on problems pertaining to their own units or vacation needs. The board is required to poll the owners prior to implementing major changes, and majority vote rules.

The management may have the freedom to hire and fire its employees or service companies as deemed necessary to meet the quality standards set by the board. It must do so, however, within the set guidelines of the annual budget and may not incur greater expense without board approval or owner justification. This does not mean that budgets will always balance, or that an accountant is required at all times. It is not uncommon for expenses in some areas to exceed budgeted figures, since inflation will take its toll on even the best-planned budget, but a good management operation will find ways to compensate in other areas, so that owners will not have to face steady increases or suffer reduced standards.

One association decided to delete some of the frills that came with their purchases in order to fight inflation. They discontinued daily newspaper delivery and fresh flowers for every apartment each week. While this may seem insignificant, remember that the multiples begin with 51 weeks and grow in ratio to the number of apartments involved. Some amenities may be expendable without reducing overall quality when such things as utility increases cause budget problems.

WHAT IS THE COST AND COVERAGE OF MAINTENANCE?

The proposed budget for a resort can be found in the condominium documents issued by the developer. Obviously, the operations and upkeep of the resort apartments and facilities depend greatly upon an adequate budget.

A sample budget appears on page 190, and page 106 shows the actual cost to each owner of one resort that has been in operation since 1976.

The two major costs are the upkeep of the resort (inside and out) and the staff required. Fees are based on the appropriate pro rata share of each unit and then divided by the 52 weeks of operations (you'll note that even though only 50 or 51 weeks are sold, the extra week still must be figured for costing and sharing among all owners). The national average maintenance fee for timeshare units at the end of 1980 was about $130 per week per unit for upkeep, operations and amenities. That was a 30 percent increase from the national average fee two years earlier. Thus, the average fee had risen at around 12 percent per year, close to the annual inflation rate. Differences in unit size, furnishings and amenities among units of the same type account for the variations in annual fees. In a broad study, there was a marked variation based on actual management experience; resorts with three or more years of operating experience tended to have higher fees than new resorts, suggesting that new resorts had underestimated costs.

TYPICAL MAINTENANCE BUDGET
Cost Per Week of Ownership

Project a 31-unit interval ownership condominium
Size of Units: 2-bedroom, 1,300 sq. ft.

Maintenance Fees	Per Week of Occupancy
Accounting	$ .95
Association meeting and expense	1.58
Cablevision	1.45
Electricity (common areas)	2.46
Gas (pool and barbeque)	4.11
Insurance	6.96
Lawn maintenance	4.93
Maintenance service and supplies	8.22
Annual unit maintenance (painting, etc.)	3.16
Management fee	11.51
Occupational license	.06
Office supplies and postage	1.27
Payroll and related taxes	20.24
Pest control	1.45
Reserve for maintenance repairs	6.96
Reserve for depreciation	6.01
Telephone	3.06
Waste disposal	2.28
Water and sewer (common areas)	1.34
Contingency	2.00
	$ 90.00
Occupancy Fees	
Maid service (weekly)	$ 25.00
Weekly cleaning supplies	5.00
Water and sewer (unit)	9.00
Books, newspapers, magazines	3.00
Electricity (unit)	21.00
(Per diem fee—$9.00)	$ 63.00
Real estate tax (billed directly to owner)	$ 30.00
Total	$183.00

ASSESSMENTS

Another common question is "Even if my maintenance fee is only $131 this year, how do I know it won't be $250 next year?" And "How can I tell whether I'm being overcharged or not?"

The simple answer is that in a properly run interval resort, the board will have set limits on the amount by which annual maintenance fees can be raised without member approval. For example, some maintenance fees are tied to an index, such as the Consumer Price Index, or a 15 percent ceiling. Thus, the fee may not be raised more than the increase allowed for in the year under budget. Furthermore, as a member of the owners' association, you have a right to review the annual budget, and it may be rejected by a majority vote of the association. If the assessment is higher than allowed, the owners can call a special meeting, and not only reject the budget, but recall the board of directors as well. Even when the developer is still in control of the resort, no budget that is more than 15 percent above the prior year's budget can be adopted without the approval of a majority of owners, if that is the figure stipulated in the agreement.

There are some accounts which are exempt from those limitations. These include reserves for replacement of resort property or one-time costs (nonrecurring expenses) for improvements to the property.

And, of course, the annual audit of the association's accounts by an independent accounting firm must be made available to any member three months after the fiscal year has ended.

Maintenance budgets cover all of the known expenses to provide everything the resort needs for the coming year; security, utilities, taxes, lawn care, pool service, maid service, annual and general maintenance, replacement reserves for furnishings and equipment, management fee, personnel salaries and taxes, insect control, repairs and replacement of damaged equipment and recreational facilities. The expenses of the association are also included—items such as postage, telephones, stationery and meetings. If your resort has individual telephone service in the apartment, the monthly phone bills are included in the budget, but each owner is responsible for long distance charges during his week of occupancy.

Management decisions as to bulk purchasing of items such as pool chemicals, lawn fertilizer and insecticides through competitive bidding can go a long way in minimizing the increases in costs that are bound to come. It is up to the officers and directors of the association to see that those management refinements are part of the resort's operating policy. Just because the brother-in-law of the project manager is in the pool supply business, it doesn't mean he has the best prices. Get several bids for all such supplies.

Even if inflation causes some budget hikes, you'll only notice a small increase, because you're sharing this responsibility with all the other owners on a pro rata basis. And if the cost of owning by the week sounds steep, it merely reflects the overall cost increases for the entire condominium.

Maintenance fees are usually due in the first quarter of every year, which means a tremendous flood of cash comes into the bank all at once. Since the cash flow must cover the entire year, most associations place a significant balance of these funds in an interest-earning account or a guaranteed trust plan. The earnings from this investment belong to the association and can help to defray inflation's impact or be used for improvements approved by the owners.

WHAT ABOUT WILLFUL DAMAGE AND THEFT?

Amazingly, the amount of damage and pilferage in interval resorts is so minimal that most associations don't regard it as a problem. There are two very good reasons for that. First, pride of ownership and a desire to maintain an excellent vacation home prevail among owners and guests. Secondly, both the condominium declarations and the lease provide that if something is missing or damaged after you visit, you are responsible for the replacement charges. Before you check in, the project housekeeper will inspect the unit. In every unit, the same items are in pretty much the same location. The housekeeper can "eyeball" the unit in a matter of minutes, use the checklist and determine if all is as it should be. If the previous occupant walked out with the AM/FM radio, it will be replaced by the maid or service man. Your predecessor will be denied future access to the resort and will be in default to the resort until the bill is paid. It's difficult to say whether it's the result of a fierce pride of ownership or the financial penalties that will be incurred but theft and damage are seldom problems in these resorts.

THEN THERE'S NORMAL WEAR AND TEAR

There's not much that can be done about cigarette burns on the coffee table or Bloody Mary stains on the beige carpet—that's considered part of the normal wear and tear in the apartments. Nicks and scuffs appear in your vacation apartment just as they do at home, and as long as willful negligence is not the case, there will be no extra charges levied against the occupant. Part of the annual budget is set aside for repairs and cleaning of this nature.

One area of concern from people in the industry is whether the reserve fund for replacement of major items will be sufficient to compete with deflated buying power several years down the road. Obviously, everything in the apartments will need repair or replacement some day, and projecting long-range budgets for some of the major items is one of the most difficult chores facing management today.

Most resorts are now spending from $8,000 to $18,000 per unit for the initial furnishing and decor package. If inflation continues on its present path of 10 to 12 percent per year, those replacements will cost $16,000 to $36,000 in ten years or so, when most items will need to be replaced or undergo major overhaul.

Fortunately, all replacement problems won't occur at the same time, but even staggered year by year, the reserves might not pay the bill at the appropriate time. But, again, your share as an individual owner will indeed be minimal when divided among all the other owners of the unit. In this light, it is much less of a problem.

RULES AND REGULATIONS OF THE OWNERS' ASSOCIATION

In addition to being responsible for the resort budget, the owners' association also writes the rules that owners and their guests must follow while using the units. Some of the rules may seem rather strict at first, but it is important to remember that many families will be using the one apartment throughout the year. Thus, for the safety and enjoyment of all owners and for the preservation of the property, certain minimal rules of behavior are required.

The association also sets rules regarding late payment of fees and hours during which owners may check in and out of their units.

WHAT CAN CHANGE IN THE FUTURE?

If it's an old resort that has been converted to timesharing, the association should receive, or have access to, the building's "mechanicals," such as heating and air conditioning systems, plumbing, wiring and swimming pool construction. The developer has probably made other improvements that management will need to know about, since they may affect future budgets or require separate attention.

With a new building, these same concerns may not exist, but the association will need to evaluate the materials used and estimate the duration of their use. If, for example, a building is centrally air conditioned and a roof mount "chiller" goes out, the owners are going to get a pretty hefty bill for the replacement. So management should make certain that the building products being used are of good quality and that the proper warranties and service contracts to protect the owners from additional expenses are in force.

Developers interviewed for this book made it quite clear that they are in business to stay, to do a good job and to give what they promise and, they hope, just a bit more. They realize the importance of good management and maintenance, and they agree that the ultimate success and longevity of resort timesharing will depend as much upon the quality of their operation as it will upon the beauty of the structure and surroundings.

CHAPTER 5

Worldwide Exchange Networks: The Icing on the Cake?

Most major resorts belong to one of the two leading exchange networks or may be a part of a separate chain with its own international exchange program. The flexibility and versatility provided by exchange to other vacation areas and at other times of the year is a tremendous asset for the buyer. By virtue of the exchange networks, it is now possible for you to swap with owners at almost 400 resorts on five continents, depending upon the network your resort selects. While the greatest number are located in the United States, you may be able to enjoy the shimmering blue waters of the Caribbean, the hills and beaches of Mexico, the sparkling snows of the Swiss Alps, the canals of Venice, the sights of London.

And the best part of exchanging is that your new accommodations are almost rent free. As long as your annual dues are paid and you can afford the nominal exchange fee, you have only to offer for exchange your resort accommodation.

HOW EXCHANGING WORKS

Because the exchange network derives its income solely from arranging trades, its ultimate success depends on its ability to serve its clients. The addition of more resorts to those already functioning in prime vacation areas provides the exchange network with more potential exchange inventory.

Today, thanks to computers, trades can be made among hundreds of participants without requiring direct interchange between "A" and "B." Simply put, member A can swap to B while B trades to C and C may want to vacation at Z—with Z's owner perhaps completing the chain of exchanges by going to A's resort. If there are no units available at the resort you ask for, alternatives are usually suggested. The exchange network allows you to see a different resort in your area or a different time period in resorts with availabilities, and you may reject alternatives until you find something that appeals to you. No square pegs are forced into round holes. And there is no charge unless you confirm an exchange.

Once you decide to trade a week, simply mail in the trade request form or call the toll-free number of the exchange network, giving them the information they'll need to process your exchange:

1. in order of priority, your three desired vacation *areas*
2. specific resorts in those areas you had in mind
3. the dates you prefer and possible alternate dates
4. the number of adults and children in your party

5. the sleeping capacity needed (not to exceed the number you have in your unit)
6. the name of your resort, unit number and week number offered for exchange

You may get immediate confirmation, or you may have to wait because, as with the airlines, openings fluctuate greatly—by the day, or even by the hour. Exchange networks will require you to notify them of your desire to trade at least 60 days prior to your home resort vacation time or the requested date, whichever comes first. And you'd be wise to give them as much advance notice as possible. However, in fairness to all, networks will not accept trade requests more than 12 months in advance. Once your request is received, it is placed into the network's computer along with the week you are providing for exchange. The computer takes it from there, seeking a match for your first choice of resort, time and unit size. If a match is found, your trade is confirmed. If no match can be found, the network will either keep looking or let you know their best alternatives, depending on your instructions.

WHO ARE THE EXCHANGE NETWORKS?

Resort Condominiums International (RCI) was the first network on the scene, the brainchild of a talented husband and wife team, Christel and Jon DeHaan in Indianapolis, Indiana. The DeHaans originally conceived RCI in 1974 to assist the floundering condominium developer in selling new units, and as a viable service to owners who wanted to exchange their wholly owned condominiums on occasion for variety in vacations. The DeHaans' timing couldn't have been better, for RCI soon found itself right in the middle of the newly born interval resort sharing industry.

As of July 1981, RCI had more than 130,000 members

at over 480 resorts located in 30 countries under exchange representation agreement, both wholly owned and interval types. About 400 of these resorts have a majority of interval or exchange units; the total number of apartments listed by RCI is about 12,000. Multiply this by the 51 weeks of interval use and you arrive at an impressive total of 612,000 unit weeks! Even keeping in mind that some units in either network are presently under construction, in renovation or still in planning stages, the figures are impressive. These units should be ready for occupancy in one to three years. Of course, unit weeks are often purchased in multiples, but there will still be thousands of opportunities for exchange.

Interval International (I.I.) was the second major exchange, following RCI some 18 months later in 1976. It is based in Miami, Florida. It's principal founders were Thomas J. Davis, Jr., a Miami attorney, and Mario Rodriguez, a former accountant, who saw the need for a second and competitive exchange network.

According to I.I.'s latest figures, they have exchange agreements with over 270 resorts specializing in timesharing in 30 countries. Using the same multiples as for RCI, I.I. would have about 11,200 interval apartments offering about 571,200 unit weeks.

Both networks are extremely efficient and fully capable of honoring their commitments to their members. While other networks have been formed and more may enter the field, at the time of this writing none has yet attained the volume of business of these two. Some major developers with several resorts do provide their own internal exchange services while still retaining membership in one of these major networks. American International Vacations, Royal Aloha and Sweetwater Properties are among the most noted in this category, with very favorable reports from their members.

Since the two major networks play such an important role in this new industry, I will describe their basic exchange guidelines for members.

HOW TO ENJOY THEIR EXPANDING ALTERNATIVES
Resort Condominiums International (RCI)

Subscription requirements: New owners of resort sharing units are eligible to join RCI, and the $100 initial membership fee will be waived if the annual calendar-year subscription dues of $39 are paid at the time of purchase. The added $100 fee will be charged should you choose to join at a later time, but normally the developer pays the first year's membership fee. RCI requires only one membership fee regardless of the number of weeks or number of resorts controlled by the listed owner; membership is nontransferable. Should you sell a unit week at one of your resorts, you may transfer the unused portion of your membership to the new buyer.

Exchange operations: Buyers whose units are not available for use at the time of purchase because of construction, renovation or refurbishing will be enrolled; they will receive all RCI benefits except the exchange privilege. When the unit is ready for occupancy, trades can be made.

When two or more parties residing at different addresses purchase jointly, each *must* enroll, should membership be desired; co-owners are responsible for coordinating their exchange powers and transactions.

Membership for a corporation will be in the name of the corporate officer and company; additional employees authorized to utilize exchange privileges must become individual members, but the $100 membership fee is waived.

RCI categorizes unit weeks into color-keyed exchange priority divisions: red = greater demand, white = average demand and blue = lesser demand. Trades within their matching demand or color period are the norm. Requests for downgrades (when a prime week is traded for an average or lesser week) will be granted, but requests for upgrades will not. Nor are members allowed to request a trade for a unit with more sleeping space than the one they deposited.

RCI works on a Spacebank deposit and withdrawal system, similar to your savings account. To withdraw, you first must deposit your vacation time at least 60 days before your own unit is available, then you can withdraw the desired time 45 days prior to the first day of the month requested. You may deposit as many weeks as you wish and may cancel any portion at any time, if it has not been assigned and you have not traveled against this deposit. RCI notifies you and your resort only if your time has been assigned; if you don't receive notification that your unit has been assigned 21 days before your week comes up, you may use your unit and still exchange. If yours is a "floating week," you must obtain written confirmation from your resort on the confirmed reservation time you control, prior to a trade request. In summary, the person trading can still receive his desired trade elsewhere but take advantage of using/renting his own unit if the RCI is unable to use it. Owner's use does not hinder his chance for exchange; he still may not get his desired trade, however, since it may not be available sometime in the future. In such case, he has at least not been denied use of his unit nor missed a vacation opportunity.

A toll-free service is available to members who have deposited time but don't know when they will be able to take their vacations until 30 to 44 days from the day of their call. Availabilities can be confirmed at that time, and confirmation will be received after RCI's receipt of the normal exchange fee ($38 per week involved) or a major credit card number.

RCI provides an accrual program to allow members to save on vacation weeks that would otherwise be lost because a vacation unit was not used. If the unit was placed in the Spacebank and used by RCI but no exchange was requested against this deposit, the owner may use the exchange the next year. However, he may not piggyback the accrued weeks with the next year's weeks at the same

EXCHANGE REQUEST FORM

(Vacation Time Request)

Please type or print clearly

RCI Membership I.D.# 0008-9999

Name: John Harvey

Address: 2002 W. Main St.

City: Somerset

State: Indiana   Zip 46233

Country: U.S.A.

Home phone: 317, 896-5000

Bus. phone: 317, 896-4999

VACATION TIME SPACEBANKED® (this does not Spacebank® your time)

I deposited my vacation time from Aruba Beach Club resort

for the dates of May 10-17 , week # 19

Year 1980 Unit # or name 244

Size of unit 1Br. Occupancy 5
(hotel unit) (eff) (1-2-3 br) (other)

TIME DIVISION DEPOSITED:
___RED   X WHITE   ___BLUE

See facilities chart to find the color code of *your* vacation time dates.

MY 1st CHOICE FOR AN EXCHANGE REQUEST IS AREA:

① ② ③ ④ Ⓧ ⑥ ⑦ ⑧ ⑨ ⑩ ⑪ ⑫ ⑬ ⑭ ⑮ ⑯ ⑰ ⑱
(geographical areas #1 — #18)

PLEASE CHOOSE 2 RESORTS FROM ONE AREA AND NOT TWO FROM THE SAME CITY.

PREFERRED RESORT: #1: The Wren

PREFERRED RESORT: #2: Iron Blosam

MONTHS: The color of vacation time deposited *must match* the color of the time requested.

Jan.		May		Sept.
Feb.		June	X	Oct.
Mar.		July	X	Nov.
Apr.		Aug.		Dec.

Preferred date: June 13-20, 1980

MY 2nd CHOICE FOR AN EXCHANGE REQUEST IS AREA:

① ② ③ ④ ⑤ ⑥ ⑦ ⑧ ⑨ ⑩ ⑪ ⑫ Ⓧ ⑭ ⑮ ⑯ ⑰ ⑱
(geographical areas #1 — #18)

PLEASE CHOOSE 2 RESORTS FROM ONE AREA AND NOT TWO FROM THE SAME CITY.

PREFERRED RESORT: #1: Royal Kuhio

PREFERRED RESORT: #2: Kona Billfisher

I will be: Driving ☐
    Renting a car ☐
    Flying ☒

Which is more important to you? Area ___ X

Activities or interests: swimming, sightseeing

Number of persons in my party: 4 adults 2 children 2

MONTHS: The color of vacation time deposited *must match* the color of the time requested.

Jan.		May		Sept.
Feb.		June	X	Oct.
Mar.		July	X	Nov.
Apr.		Aug.		Dec.

Preferred date: June 14-21, 1980

Time ___

IMPORTANT:

1. If the information on your Exchange Request form is incomplete or incorrect RCI will return the form to you.

2. When exchanging, the number of persons in your party cannot exceed the occupancy limits of your own unit nor the occupancy limits of the resort to which you will be confirmed.

3. Your exchange request form must be received by RCI at the very least forty-five (45) days prior to the first day of the earliest month you are requesting [sixty (60) days for International Exchanges].

4. For each week requested, enclose your $28 (710 Pesos or 15£) exchange fee check payable to RCI.

Date: 1/30/80   RCI Member *John Harvey*
(Signature)

PLEASE SUBMIT EARLY. FOR EACH WEEK REQUESTED, ENCLOSE $28 (710 PESOS OR 15£) PAYABLE TO RCI FOR EXCHANGE FEES.

MEMBERSHIP DUES MUST BE PAID FOR THE YEAR IN WHICH YOU ARE REQUESTING AN EXCHANGE.

Please send check drawn on a U.S. Bank or remit 20% above required amount when paying in foreign currency.

RCI© Copyright January 1, 1980

119

resort. In short, RCI believes that no member should expect to "trade something for nothing," and trades are restricted by both occupancy size of the unit and the seasonal priority levels. Therefore, if the owner's week(s) are used by someone else and he has not yet been confirmed anywhere (availabilities may not be open), he won't be left holding an empty bag and miss out on a vacation. But an owner/member should not expect unlimited abilities to exchange.

Interval International (I.I.)

Subscription requirements: New resort purchasers are eligible to join at the annual fee of $39 within 90 days of their transaction. Should they elect not to join within that time, they must wait four years for reapplication. There is no other initial membership fee. I.I. requires either a membership for *each* resort in cases of multiple-resort purchases by one family or offers a $50 master membership to cover all. Membership is transferable should an owner sell a unit week and wish to include the balance of membership time in the sale. It is not transferable if he still retains weeks at that resort. Computation of a 12-month membership begins on the day the application and fee is processed at I.I.; it is renewable on its anniversary date or within 90 days without penalty.

Members may not exchange until such time as their home resort unit is occupiable, but all other benefits may be exercised.

When two or more joint owners reside at different addresses, one individual will control responsibility for their resort unit.

Membership for a corporation is the same as for an individual, except that the corporate officer may allocate use or trade as he sees fit and no additional memberships are required for employees.

Exchange Operations: I.I. does not categorize unit weeks into priority divisions, and members are free to upgrade or downgrade as long as their request is not for more sleeping capacity than they are relinquishing in trade. Exceptions may be made if all the units in the requested resort are the same type, and weeks are available.

I.I. does not work on a banking system but does operate on the "you must give up a week to get a week" method. Exchange requests can be handled entirely by toll-free phone calls; you must allow at least 60 days before your home resort date and the new date/resort requested. You may place your weeks for trade as far as a year in advance, by phone or in writing, with the option of selecting an area for your own use later. Or you may refuse the incoming trade until up to 37 days in advance of your own unit week's start date. After that, your participation in a swap, due to the short period of time available for I.I. to find a user for your week, may be on a discretionary basis. Although I.I. does not set priority criteria as a restrictive tool, it does accept shorter notice on prime weeks simply because it knows a user will surface faster than on less popular weeks.

Floating weeks also require resort time confirmation prior to a trade request.

The I.I. cost for trading is $39 *per trip transaction*, regardless of how many weeks are involved at one time. Consecutive weeks at another resort, regardless of the timing of the weeks, constitute one trip transaction. A request for two different resorts constitutes two trip transactions and costs $39 for each. There is no accrual system, but exchanges can be made within the 12-month membership period, rather than within a calendar year basis.

THE EXCHANGE NETWORKS' RESORT LOCATIONS

The following list represents the city or region of all the resorts currently belonging to both exchange networks; you'll note that almost every state in the Union has at least one resort and the more vacation-oriented climes are heavily populated with them. The same holds true for many other continents. For the sake of space, the names of the more than 600 resorts are not included; these may be obtained directly from the networks.

UNITED STATES

Alabama
Gulf Shores

Arizona
Pinetop
Scottsdale
Show Low

Arkansas
Eureka Springs
Fairfield Bay

California
Fallbrook
Indio
Laguna Beach
Lake Tahoe
Palm Springs
Ramona
San Diego

Colorado
Breckenridge
Crested Butte
Dillon
Durango
Estes Park
Frisco
Garfield
Marble
Silverthorne
Snowmass
Steamboat
   Springs
Vail
Winter Park

Florida
Boca Raton
Captiva
Clearwater
Cocoa Beach
Daytona
Delray
Estero Island
Everglades City
Fort Lauderdale
Fort Myers Beach
Hillsboro Beach
Hollywood
Hutchison Island
Islamorada
Jupiter
Kissimmee
Lehigh
Longboat Key
Lower
   Matecumbe
Marathon
Miami Beach
Naples
Orlando
Ormond Beach
Pensacola
St. Petersburg
Sanibel Island
Sarasota
Satellite Beach
Sebastian
South Shores
Tampa

Treasure Island
Vero Beach

Georgia
Dillard
Villa Rica

Idaho
Blanchard
Henry's Lake
Ketchum
Lava Hot Springs
Macks
McCall
Sun Valley

Kentucky
Burnside
Woodson Bend

Louisiana
New Orleans

Maine
East Stoneham
Greenville

Maryland
Annapolis
Ocean City

Massachusetts
Cape Cod
Martha's
   Vineyard
Nantucket
South Lee

Michigan

Boyne Falls
Harbor Springs
Mancelona
Traverse City

Minnesota

Hill City
Park Rapids

Mississippi

Lumberton

Missouri

Kimberling City
Lake Ozark
Lampe

Montana

Big Sky
Kalispell
Pray
West Yellowstone

Nevada

Incline Village
Lake Tahoe
Las Vegas
Reno
Stateline
Zephyr Cove

New Hampshire

Ashland
Campton
Franconia
Glen
Laconia
Lincoln
North Conway
Weirs Beach
Wolfeboro

New Jersey

Atlantic City
McAfee

New Mexico

Angel Fire
Chama
Cloudcroft
Ruidoso
Santa Fe
Santa Teresa

North Carolina

Asheville
Banner
Blowing Rock
Boone
Elk
Lake Lure
Murphy
New Bern
Whispering Pines

Oregon

Sunriver

Pennsylvania

Albrightsville
Bushkill
Dingman's Ferry
Lackawaxen
Mount Pocono
Shawnee

Rhode Island

Charlestown

South Carolina

Hilton Head
Myrtle Beach

Tennessee

Crossville
Fairfield Glade
Gatlinburg
Lake Palestine

Texas

Austin
Bridgeport
Brownsville
Conroe
Corpus Christi
Freeport
Huntsville
Lago Vista
Marble Falls
Montgomery
Padre Island

Utah

Brigham City
Fairview
Garden City
Park City
St. George
Snowbird

Vermont

Brownsville
Quechee
Stowe
Warren

Virginia

Bayse
Harrisonburg
Virginia Beach

Washington

Birch Bay
Glacier
Manson
Ocean City
Ocean Park

Washington,
continued

Ocean Shores
Port Townsend
Snoquaimie Pass
Union

Wisconsin

Eagle River
Green Lake
Lake Geneva

Wyoming

Jackson Hole

HAWAIIAN ISLANDS

Hawaii

Kona
Pahala

Kauai

Kapaa

Maui

Kaamapala
Kahena
Kihei

Oahu

Honolulu
Makaha
Waikiki

CANADA

Alberta

Cranmore

British Columbia

Caribou
Fairmont
   Hot Springs

Kelowna
Victoria Island
Whistler

Manitoba

Falcon Lake

Ontario

Barrie
Gananoque

Quebec

Bromont
Monte St. Anne

MEXICO

Acapulco
Cancun
Cozumel
Cuernavaca

Guaymas
Manzanillo
Mazatlan
Puerto Vallarta

Santiago
Taxco
Vera Cruz

CARIBBEAN

Bahamas

Cable Beach
Freeport
Nassau

British West
Indies

Grenadines

Jamaica

Montego Bay
Ocho Rios

Puerto Rico

Fajardo
Humacao
San Juan

Virgin Islands

St. Croix
St. Thomas
Tortolo

EUROPE

Belgium

Knikke-LeZoute

England

Devon
Torquay

France

Auron
Megeve
Menton
Port Leucate

Savoie
Villeneuve

Italy

Marilleva
Monteriggioni
Oliveri
Sardinia

Scotland

Fife
Perthshire

Spain

Cadiz
Ibiza
Marbella
Menorca
Mojacar

Switzerland

Montana

Wales

Pennal

OTHERS

Australia

Coffs Harbour
Phillips Island
Port Macquarie
Queensland
Sydney
Tuncurry
West Greenough

Chile

El Colorado
Renaca

Fiji

Nadi
Queenstown
Wairakei

Israel

Tiberias

Mariana Islands

Guam
Saipan

New Zealand

Picton

Philippines

Baguio City

Polynesia

Bora Bora

Venezuela

Puerto La Cruz

SOME TIPS ON TRADING

Of course, people with prime weeks at first-class resorts will enjoy an advantage in trading because they can
control the availability of their units until they are happy
with the exchange they have been given in return. Still,
there is plenty of opportunity for good exchanges for people with more moderate units to offer.

An executive of one of the exchange networks points
out that he doesn't like to talk about their "success rate"
because it can be so misleading. He says

If we tell our members that our success rate of overall exchanges to requests is 80 percent, they'll think they have an 80 percent chance of getting any trade they want. And that's really not true. The family with a prime ski week has virtually 100 percent chance of getting the trade it wants, while someone with a really off-season (usually spring and fall) unit may have only a 20 percent chance, depending upon the week he seeks in return.

Thus, the key to a successful exchange is to have a realistic understanding of the system, a mind open to alternatives, and a flexible schedule. Your goal, after all, is to have an unusual and enjoyable vacation that meets your expectations. Members who are prepared to allow modification of their plans will get the most use and satisfaction out of the exchange program.

Furthermore, only a few of the 225,000 members in both exchange networks may seek a trade each year. At this time, the industry is too young for us to be able to chart any significant trends as to when members will trade. If you're really sold on your resort and location, it may be many years before wanderlust sets in; or you may want to trade every few years. A member who has just recently purchased his interval unit is likely to use it exclusively for the next several years. Experts predict that the real boom in exchanging will begin in the mid-1980s, after a greater number of members have become more familiar with their own resorts and local facilities.

Both exchange networks keep track of figures indicating how many trade requests are received on a quarterly basis and how many are fulfilled. Generally, their success rate has been in the 75 percent to 85 percent range.

In a study prepared for the National Timesharing Council early in 1980 from a sampling of members who purchased from some of the major developers in the industry, nearly 37 percent said they had requested a trade at one time or another. That means that 63 percent had never sought to exchange. Of those who did, almost 90 percent said they were "satisfied" or "very satisfied" with the handling and results of their trade. Considering that the two networks processed 21,700 requests in 1979, they appear to be doing an admirable job. One warning, however; only 36 percent received confirmation of their first choice of resorts. The satisfaction levels indicate that their alternate selections were more than adequate in spite of initial unavailability.

If your resort is not very exciting and lacks the leisure activities that would entice you to return, don't expect it to have high exchange demand. However, if the vacation package is good and in a popular area, you can expect adequate action in the exchange market; you will also find it easier to rent your unit if you aren't going to use it every year.

Earlier we included a calendar on how the unit weeks are numbered. While each trade network gives individual weeks and months different priority classifications and while there can be exceptions, there are enough similarities for us to provide the following chart:

Weeks in This Season	Ranking
Christmas to Easter	Prime exchange capability
Easter to Memorial Day	Low exchange priority
Memorial Day to Labor Day	Good to prime exchange capability for many resort areas
Labor Day to Christmas	Low exchange priority

The vacation habits and timetables of the public establish prime times for resorts. Periods when children are out of school are among the best—Christmas, Easter, summer vacations or long holidays—as are those periods when skiing is best. Southern climes are busiest when winter becomes unbearable in the north. Because the "interval calendar" differs from the regular calendar, July 4th may appear in week 26 one year and week 27 the next. The fall foliage season in New England or race week in Daytona or Mardi Gras in New Orleans all qualify as prime times. But beware—they usually don't fall within the same week, year after year. Easter falls sometimes in March and other years in April. The foliage season can be as unpredictable on a calendar as fresh powder at a ski resort.

Be sure to know the networks' evaluation of the unit weeks you want to buy or check with the local chamber of commerce to compare tourism peaks and valleys. While a developer may say that you are buying a week with above-average trade capability, and his calculations may support this, exchangers from other parts of the country may not support it with their all-important requests for exchange.

HOW TO ENJOY THEIR EXPANDING SERVICES

Both networks are similar in wanting to satisfy as many requests for trades as they possibly can; their profit depends on volume and, aside from annual memberships, their only other major income derives from exchange fees.

Both networks can also handle exchange within your own resort, allowing you the flexibility of enjoying your resort at times you didn't purchase. You may vacation at a lake in New Hampshire in the summer one year, but want to witness fall in all its glory at the same resort via exchange.

Both networks require additional time, at least 60 to 90 days, to handle trades in foreign countries. You can travel to faraway places like South Africa, Japan, Australia and Israel, but it is a little more complicated to arrange exchanges.

The networks have agreements whereby developers will provide them with a percentage of unsold unit weeks during the marketing period and thereby expand the exchange capability and potential of newer resorts.

Both have advanced computer technology to keep pace with their accelerating growth; they are well staffed, and have offices overseas for liaison with their members and with new resorts.

Being a member of a network offers other benefits you may find of value. You'll receive mailings, including a colorful magazine, four to six times a year, updating information on new and existing resorts as well as introducing those recently approved in the final planning stages. By keeping track of resort growth in areas of interest to you, you'll be able to plan long-range vacation schedules beneficial to you and the network. You'll receive annually a comprehensive and colorful directory that profiles the resorts and area attractions in greater detail. With this vacation "yearbook," you'll be able to select future exchanges at resorts or areas that appeal to your spirit of adventure. These publications also detail any changes in policy and describe new membership benefits.

More recently, the networks have added rental car discounts, travel insurance policies, lost-luggage- and credit-card-tracer services and informative brochures on amenities in the area surrounding your selected exchange resort. Currency exchange information, emergency cash forwarding, additional lodging discounts and coupon books also add to the "travel club" atmosphere.

The major feature, of course, is still the flexibility and variety offered by interval resort exchange.

DON'T EXPECT MIRACLES NOR BUY SOLELY FOR THE EXCHANGE

Before a resort is admitted to one of the networks, it must pass a rigid 65-point inspection covering everything from the ambiance and interior/exterior of the facilities to the financial security of the developer. Tourist trends of the area and the ratio of in-season weeks to off-season weeks are carefully weighed; this is the part of the evaluation that can cause the network headaches later on, should they err in computing the exchange potential of a resort.

The networks do a conscientious job in keeping low-standard applicants from achieving "status" through admission; rejections have increased substantially now that the networks have reached a level where they can be scrupulous in setting industry standards. Thus, they wield considerable power in their ability to exclude second-rate developments from interval resort sharing. Similarly, the networks can expel resorts that fail to live up to the set standards. Public response has proven that a resort must provide the exchange option in order to compete successfully. So resort developers know that consumer protection comes not only by way of governmental intervention, but also from within their own affiliated private business sectors that demand certain standards be set and maintained.

I mention this not because I want to heap roses on the exchange networks (although they are doing fine work), but to show that most of the time there are effective checks and balances which will assist you in making an informed decision about the interval vacation concept.

Nothing is foolproof, and once in a while a resort slips through that just doesn't make it financially or doesn't have very strong exchange appeal. Then, trading out becomes a disappointment. That's why you must learn everything you can about your resort to make sure that, if the worst were to happen, you could vacation there (at the time periods you select) for many years to come and be happy. Don't expect the exchange networks to perform miracles because you're unhappy with your resort or time period selection. They've done their best to protect the public, but they can't oversee the sales operation or management of your resort. They can only applaud from the sidelines when a resort fulfills its potential and, through frequent visits to the resort, determine if their standards are being maintained for exchange members.

Too often, uninformed buyers have thought they could beat the system: buy the most inexpensive week and trade for prime-time units in other popular resort areas. If a sales representative implies that you can swap for just about any resort you want at any time of the year, be wary of his business practices. *It can't be done!* You might be lucky once or twice, but for the most part you'll be left with your own unit year after year. What the exchange networks are saying is that even with the best week in the calendar, they can't promise you 100 percent trade satisfaction.

The solution is quite simple. If you intend to exchange with any regularity, buy the more popular (and expensive) unit weeks. If your resort is in a highly popular tourist area and has that special touch of class, there will be a demand for your unit week. Just as you would have no trouble renting your unit week, you will also be able to arrange excellent exchanges.

Now, I don't want to imply that you won't be happy with a lower-priced, less-in-demand unit week. On the contrary, buyers of the more economical weeks can enjoy vacation variety and flexibility just as much as those who pay more. It's a matter of personal preference. A lot of families prefer vacations during the more quiet times when resort areas are less busy; when the weather is cooler or in transition. They prefer to exchange abroad when they're not shoulder to shoulder with tourists. And there are areas that have virtually no seasonal variation —areas like Hawaii, Las Vegas or the Caribbean. There is still plenty of variety and flexibility for the knowledgeable owner who can be flexible himself. Trading within your own season or time period usually will prove more successful, thanks to continual efforts by the networks to upgrade their facilities and services.

The networks have done their homework well and, for the most part, the exchange resort vacations you'll experience in new, untried areas may be even better than you had hoped for.

SOME ADVANTAGES AND LIMITATIONS

Here are a few more points to consider:

Advantages of the Exchange

1. No matter what the value of your unit, a job transfer doesn't leave you out on a limb; if you choose, you can exchange for resort areas closer to your new location every year as long as you follow the network's guidelines. If you owned a second home or expensive vacation condo, your investment would force you either to return to it yearly or to sell it.
2. You have a quality-control watchdog in the network, keeping developers on their toes.
3. You don't have to join or renew; this is strictly voluntary on your part.
4. If you're an owner at a resort, chances are good that your equity interest gives you a voice in keeping or replacing your association's choice of exchange networks.
5. If your developer is one of the few who is expelled from or becomes inactive in a network, you may still be able to exchange. The networks will continue to honor your membership as long as the resort still meets network standards and if your own dues are paid.

Limitations of the Exchange

1. You can't exchange until your home unit is ready for occupancy; since most families buy into new resorts for the following year's vacation, an occupancy delay beyond your next year's time would negate use or trade of your time until the following year.
2. You are financially responsible, in most resorts,

for major damages caused by exchangers using your unit; however, the instances of this have been minuscule since few members will risk personal expulsion from the network as a "poor trade risk."

3. Generally, you can't house more people in your exchange than you could at your home unit; this restriction is somewhat flexible, since some resorts only have larger units and are approved for more use by the network. This restriction was instituted to discourage "beating the system"—buying the smallest unit and continually trying to upgrade to larger ones. The exchange networks want to maintain trading systems that give everyone a fair shot at all the good resorts.

4. You can't exchange to the same resort two years in a row; again, this has been designed to keep a few from monopolizing the best resorts.

5. To date there is not enough data to predict the ease or difficulty of exchange—or the ability of the networks to handle a mass onslaught of trade requests satisfactorily.

6. Any significant move by the population of prime week owners to rent out their units, rather than exchange them, could greatly decrease exchange opportunities.

For the most part, exchanges work very well. The networks report that 75 to 85 percent of requests have been filled, and that 90 percent of these resulted in good trades. The odds are impressive. Of course, errors do occur, and vacationers are occasionally inconvenienced. Unlike at a motel, however, if you can't get satisfaction from the resort management, you have a ready ear in the form of the exchange network which wants you to be happy with the exchange. Your contentment means repeat business for them. Repetitious complaints mean they've got an affiliated resort that must either shape up or be expelled from the network for being substandard. But problems are rare, and you can contact your network representative for help. The networks provide an excellent service, one that will please you immeasurably.

CHAPTER 6

Buying in a Foreign Country

Thanks to the influence of Freddie Laker's low-cost "sky-train" approach to flying and the new deregulation of airline price controls and operations, the public can travel to many more vacation lands with greater speed, comfort and often less cost than by driving to old vacation spots. With the addition of interval resort sharing and the exchange networks, more families will be setting out to enjoy the foreign lands they've read about but have never been able to afford. And vacationers have begun to purchase unit weeks outside their countries. In the United States, the number of foreign families buying interval units has been on a marked increase since 1979. The strength of the U.S. real estate market, our modest inflation by world standards, and American savvy in catering to foreign visitors has placed America in the number-one position in the industry. Our consumer protection, still being improved, is perhaps the best of all interval participating countries.

For U.S. residents, the vacation areas of Mexico, the Caribbean, Europe and even Australia are becoming popular enough to merit more than an occasional visit. The buying power of the American dollar and the lure of a resort in a foreign land may tempt you to buy an interval unit outside the U.S. The following suggestions will help you make an informed decision.

KNOW THE LAW OF THE LAND AND ITS GOVERNMENT

It's one thing to visit a foreign land, pay the going rates for accommodations, recreation and sight-seeing—and often quite another to buy a piece of property there. While old English common law prevails in many countries, there are enough differences for you to be very cautious. Some countries encourage outside investors and will go to great lengths to protect your money, while others simply do not.

Should you visit a foreign country with the idea of making it your vacation home, or if you encounter a "deal too good to pass up" while there, be sure to know the law of the land before parting with your money. Your local library, attorney, travel agent or consulate can provide you with some information before you go. Whether you're going as a tourist or to investigate real estate potential, you'll want to know the political picture in that country. Is the government in control or is there a recent history of upheaval or unrest? Has its attitude toward tourism changed in the last five years? In which direction? Does that country enjoy good diplomatic relations with yours, and do those relations seem subject to change in the near future?

The political atmosphere is vitally important. Should you encounter problems, you will have to deal with them according to the laws of that country, not yours. And in case of an abrupt upheaval in government, your property could be subject to confiscation with no legal recourse for you.

Once you've determined that the government is stable and you understand the laws, you should then examine those laws in regard to protection of your investment. Will you receive equal treatment under law with citizens of the country should you attempt legal action, or will cumbersome or obscure technicalities make seeking redress a nightmare? Regardless of whether you have a right to own an equity interest in the resort or just an undisturbable membership, know what the real estate laws are and how they can affect you. If it's equity interest you're after, determine who owns the land, and for what duration. Is there an advantage to your investment if the government owns the land on which your resort is located? If the land is owned by a private developer or company, can ownership be changed (possibly to a less scrupulous management) without your knowledge or consent? What is the financial and political strength of the developer?

KNOW THE MONETARY SYSTEM

Changing dollars into pesos or francs or vice versa can be an important factor in your decision to control unit weeks in a foreign land. Since inflation has become a worldwide epidemic, the foreign exchange rates will have a direct bearing on your decision to buy an interval unit in another country. Europeans find their dollars have increased buying power in the U.S., Canada and Mexico. Canadians and Americans find advantages in Mexico and in the Caribbean—places where they also vacation with increased frequency. In the summer of 1981, for example, Americans enjoyed an advantage of 18–20 percent in exchange with Canada.

International exchange rates are subject to frequent and mercurial fluctuations which make it very difficult to predict what might happen to exchange rates in the country of your choice. (If you *are* able to make accurate projections, you may be wasting time in your current job.) But you do want to feel as secure as possible about where you place your dollars. If your review of the political and economic factors leads to a reasonable "gut feeling" of security, then you can make your decision based on the quality of the resort and the activities offered. If you feel comfortable with what you've seen, chances are you'll be making a good decision.

KNOW THE TOURISM HISTORY AND POTENTIAL

These days, statistics are available on just about everything. And especially on tourism. In the United States, for example, chambers of commerce in tourist areas are happy to offer whatever information they have to anyone who wants it. In Canada and in other tourist-oriented countries, the governments proudly publish annual—often quarterly—reports on their tourist industry.

Understanding tourist trends is very important. Your purchase price may well be a reflection of those trends. An exceptional bargain could mean that growth optimism is waning; high or rising prices may indicate the demand is greater than the supply.

Your exchange potential may be affected by changing tourist patterns. The networks have done a lot of your homework for you; they are very careful about admitting a resort into the system because there will be an imbalance if they accept too many resorts from areas of decreasing popularity. Networks have studied tourist trends and these trends affect their grading of resorts. This information may be available from the networks only if you are a member; however, you will have access to local tourist board figures.

Your ability to sell or trade your unit weeks will be affected by future market trends. Keep in mind that a marked growth in tourism will probably encourage the development of more interval resorts. Developers, too, want to get in on a good thing. If you buy in an average resort today just because it's the only one in the area, make sure it has plenty to offer vacationers, because it is very likely that the next resort to enter the picture will concentrate on providing better facilities. Naturally, if new resorts don't compare favorably with yours, you are in an enviable position for your own use, or for rentals, resales and exchanges.

When buying in a foreign land you must ask yourself whether it's an area where you'll be able to vacation frequently. Are the management and maintenance up to your standards? Is the service consistently good? How adaptable are you to the language, customs, food, services and other features of the country? Families renting or exchanging into your resort probably can adapt to any peculiarities once, but you'll be the most affected in the long run.

YOU MAY BENEFIT UNEXPECTEDLY FROM THE ADVANTAGES

Many resorts in distant lands offer wonderful vacations and sound financial investment, even though it may take time for you to fully appreciate what your "adopted home" has to offer. An already enjoyable resort will be even more valuable if plans call for the addition of a new recreational activity. In the United States, for instance, the popularity of Disney World in Florida has generated an unprecedented flurry of interval resort development to meet the demand for accommodations. Foreign visitors, after spending a great deal to reach Disney World, appreciate the savings and recreational facilities available at local interval resorts.

Tourism is big business in countries like Mexico, Canada and the Bahamas, and their governments participate actively in expanding tourist facilities. They are equally enthusiastic about the concept of interval resorts. As competition for tourist dollars increases, the advantages of high occupancy and repeat tourism created by interval resorts is very attractive to progressive governments. The same holds true for the local communities that rely heavily upon tourism for survival. Interval resorts' elimination of the peaks and valleys of tourism into a steadier year-round flow is highly desirable to the local economy. And the taxes paid by interval resorts give a tremendous lift to community budgets.

One question you may ask when considering a foreign purchase is "Am I better off buying only where my money appreciates or is on a par with the local currency?" On the surface, the answer would appear to be "Of course!" But if the rest of your research has led you to believe that you should buy, the answer could just as easily be "No!" For example, it would seem on the surface that a Canadian might be at a disadvantage buying in the U.S. in the face of a 17–20 percent exchange deficit. Statistics show that on a per capita basis, Canadians are now the most vacation-travel-oriented people in the world. So regardless of the rate of exchange, Canadians are spending their vacation dollars to enjoy what other countries have to offer. If they are renting accommodations in Florida, they willingly pay the additional exchange and are likely to pay more as increasing inflation drives costs up further. However, real estate in the U.S. over the years has proven to be a real hedge against inflation, and as long as the present value of the resort's unit weeks is acceptable, the Canadian's participation would seem to make good common sense. So he will be better off controlling or freezing his future costs for vacation accommodations through an interval purchase, even though today's price will include the foreign exchange rate.

CHAPTER 7

Should You Buy from a Local Broker?

Most interval sales have been made at the resort by resort sales personnel, because most buyers have discovered timesharing while on vacation. But as interval resort sharing becomes more commonplace, real estate brokers and their agents—whatever their location—are becoming more involved in sales. Although all forms of resort timesharing are not classified as real estate transactions and don't require licensed sales personnel (in a club membership plan, property does not change hands), real estate brokers are the most likely agents for interval resorts. Realtors have stringent consumer protection laws governing their professional ethics.

Many states are drafting legislation for the best consumer protection laws for interval resort timesharing (see the section on the NTC/NARELLO Act, Chapter 9), and they prefer that sales be made only by licensed real estate people. Since realtors must answer to both their own industry and regulatory agencies, their licenses are at stake in cases of misrepresentation of any new product or service. As long as real estate people understand the intricacies of the interval business, they will be very helpful to buyers and developers alike.

HAS HE DONE HIS HOMEWORK?

In seeking a good real estate agent, be sure he understands the mechanics of interval operations in depth and can answer your questions. He should know the various forms of interval and be able to give advice on the ones that best fit your needs, in the same manner as you'd expect him to help when buying a home. He represents the seller but has an obligation to assist you as buyer. As the middleman, he should be knowledgeable about the individual resorts—from area and resort facilities and attractions to the management and exchange network affiliation. He should have a working knowledge of unit prices, maintenance fees and financing requirements. In short, be certain he has the background necessary to help you make an intelligent decision.

SHOPPING CAN BE FUN AND INFORMATIVE

Once you've decided that you want to investigate interval vacations, your first move may be to contact a real estate agent you know. He may not have an affiliation with an interval resort but may be able to steer you to someone who does, or get pertinent information for you. If he is uninformed and unwilling to investigate timesharing for you, find another agent.

If you prefer to wait until you're on vacation to investigate the interval resorts in your favorite area, a broker can provide important information up front and save you a lot of running around to resorts that aren't suitable for you.

HOW TO OPTION YOUR PURCHASE OR ENJOY
A MINI-VACATION

If you are familiar with a resort and a broker recommends it, you may have enough information to make a final decision at that time. If the resort is unfamiliar but the broker encourages you to buy because of limited inventory or an especially good price for early purchase, ask about an option. You should not buy at a resort sight unseen unless you have the testimony of a close friend or associate whom you trust implicitly. The option merely enters you into an agreement to purchase at the set price, based upon a right of inspection and approval within the established time. The option will require paperwork and a deposit, but the transaction can be cancelled at the time of inspection and all monies, less any inspection fees, are fully refundable.

Most developers who are affiliated with off-site representation by brokers will provide a mini-vacation trip for you to inspect the resort and exercise your option. Accommodations (at or near the resort), some meals, transportation from the airport and a tour of the area are included at a nominal charge, if any. Transportation (airfare, etc.) is usually your financial responsibility but it is money well spent; you'll either make a good buy and have a mini-vacation, or you'll cancel the deal before making a big investment. Experience has proven that no matter how pretty the brochures or film presentations of a resort may be, a personal inspection is essential. Obviously, this is true if the resort doesn't live up to its advertising, but it can work the other way as well. Satisfied customers usually admit to initial hesitancy to take an option on more than one or two weeks—only to be so thoroughly delighted by the actual visit that they end up purchasing four weeks!

If you like what you see, you can make a decision on the spot. If you dislike what the inspection shows you, at least you'll be more attuned to the interval concept and better able to select a suitable resort in the future.

If you are able to shop for an interval vacation home near where you live, you will be fortunate in being able to discuss the purchase with your family before making a decision. Once again, a good agent or broker will assist you in choosing the right resort for you. Or you may find you have a decided advantage over many agents after reading this book—you've already done your homework!

CHAPTER 8

How to Plan for Resales and Rentals

Due to the fact that most timeshare purchases have been made since 1979 and the owners have been using their own units since that time, it is difficult to track rentals and resales. Developers and realtors are now receiving requests for rentals and resales, but so far there are not enough statistics available on such transactions for us to be able to predict with any certainty what you may reasonably expect. However, we can provide you with enough information to guide you in making successful resales and rentals.

HOW TO SELL YOUR WEEKS

Remember that resales may not be permitted at some right-to-use resorts, or the resort or club may have the right of first refusal, or the break-even restrictions may not motivate much interest. Owners with equity positions to offer have had the most success with resales to date. And of those, many sold privately to their friends or acquaintances although some had a little help from sales representatives. Most of our comments will apply to fee-simple, or interval ownership, sales.

Although a resale program may not benefit the developer directly, developers who assist existing owners in resale negotiations do themselves and the industry a great service.

More and more developers are beginning to see the potential for expansion in resales and are beginning to provide resale services. Additionally, state-licensed real estate brokers in major cities are acting as sales agents for timeshare projects.

In resort sales, the advertising and promotion costs are paid for by the developer; in owner resales, the broker must pay all such costs up front, before the sale is made and before he receives his commission. Few marketers or developers, caught up in the heavy expenses of completing their own resorts, have been able to assist to the degree desired by the owners.

As a resort reaches sellout, the developer's prices have risen several times as a reflection of his progress. Consequently, the owner who purchased at a lower price in the early preconstruction stage has more bargaining power in setting his resale price. If he undercuts the developer, he is entering into direct competition with him. Even if the owner matches the developer's price, it stands to reason that the developer will still want to sell his own units first, before assisting the owner in resale.

But if an owner controls the only unit or week of its kind available when a buyer is at hand, the developer will turn the sale over to the person who has a unit for resale.

Fortunately, major developers see the advantages of serving these new markets and are becoming involved in resales and rentals. The volume of paperwork required in such transactions generates in turn new support businesses—among attorneys, clerks, title insurance companies and financial institutions.

WHO CAN DO IT FOR YOU?

The best place to begin an owner's resale program is at the resort itself, among current owners who may wish to expand their vacation opportunities. Some of your time-sharing neighbors may simply want to sell their weeks in order to buy in another time frame, or they may want to put a string of weeks together for longer vacations. Others want larger units, or want to improve their exchange capabilities.

Since the resort itself can be your prime source of resale activity, how do you get representation there? If the developer is still active on site, be sure to ask him. If your resort has any affiliation with a broker to handle resales, you've overcome the first major hurdle. Then check out that affiliation to learn how effective resales have been to date and what efforts are made to assist owners wishing to sell. However, if your resort is new, the emphasis will still be on selling all resort units before considering resales. A sellout of the developer's inventory will be as advantageous to you as to the developer. You now have no competition and, chances are, the public is still coming to see what the resort is all about.

Are local brokers attuned to resort timesharing? A glimpse through the local newspaper's real estate or classified section will indicate which brokers are involved. In a resort area, most of their income derives from the sale of wholly owned condominium or oceanfront lots where the commission is in the six to seven percent range, whereas commission for timesharing is in the ten to 20 percent range but the volume of each sale is substantially lower.

Don't be alarmed if the brokers appear to have a high number of intervals for resale. When a broker has only a few weeks for sale he isn't doing a great volume of business. So he will solicit resales from owners not overly anxious to sell but who are tempted to test the marketability of their investments. Whatever the reason for his large inventory, he will probably be your best bet because he's illustrating real involvement in timesharing. One note of caution before giving him your exclusive listing: is he oversupplied with units that match yours in week number in your unit size? If your week #43 becomes the tenth for that week which he has for resale, you may want to think twice about listing your week with him. Or you may want to study the other prices when setting yours.

You may also find a broker back home who can be of service in selling your weeks. With the growth of time-sharing, realtors across the country are handling resale listings.

You can sell your interval unit yourself. Simply run a few classified ads in your local newspaper (in the real estate or travel section) or in your local weekly shopper. One of your friends, relatives or acquaintances may be interested. Tack a postcard-size announcement to the bulletin board at work or in your community center. You don't have to do any major advertising, but you may need patience to find the right buyer. Like the developer, you'll receive a lot of curiosity calls from people who don't understand what it is that you are selling.

Mortgaging for a resale buyer could be a bit difficult. To date, lending institutions feel more secure working with the developer because they have a recourse arrangement with him in cases of buyer default. Owner resales are considered to be straight consumer loans.

If you financed your original purchase and have an outstanding mortgage on your unit weeks that is nonassumable, you must either pay off this mortgage or supply your purchaser with an "agreement for deed" or try to get a "wraparound" mortgage from a new lender. The buyer can't own your weeks free and clear without receiving a recorded deed to that effect.

The resort may not be fully constructed when you decide to resell your unit week, perhaps in order to buy a different week. You can finalize this transaction quickly by issuing a purchase agreement which will suffice until the actual title has passed from the developer to you for reassignment to the buyer; after the required paperwork and recording of the deed, your buyer will have full possession and exclusive use of the weeks.

If you are anxious to sell and bank financing is not available, one way to solve the financing problem is to take back a mortgage or promissory note yourself, after receiving a down payment. An attorney can draw up the documents and include his fees in the agreement with the new buyer, or you can negotiate legal fees with the buyer at the time of the sale. The cost will vary, depending upon the intricacies of the contract, although a simple resale is fairly uncomplicated, with legal fees running anywhere from $75 to $250. And as the lender, you can defray your income for tax purposes.

Generally, the finance period is five years, although the amount of the mortgage will have some bearing on the time. Seven or ten years may be best if the amount is in the five-figure range. Your buyer will let you know what he can afford on a monthly basis and arithmetic takes it from there. At today's interest rates, you will be making good money on your mortgage.

Thus, your function is that of landlord. You have the same protection under the law as if you were selling your own home. Following due process of law, you can foreclose on a default and resume ownership of your property, retaining any amounts paid to date. Such a default is highly unlikely, however, if you have satisfied yourself on the financial qualifications of the buyer. My experience has been that interval unit resales have worked to the advantage of all concerned.

HOW TO RENT YOUR WEEKS

You will be quite free to rent your unit under interval ownership, and if you have a right-to-use membership, you probably won't be restricted from renting, although there are occasional exceptions. A club membership, vacation lease or license usually permits the transfer to others through rentals, and I pass the following information on to you with this assumption. What with competition, maintenance fees, rental commissions and the like, you probably won't make a killing on rentals, but you should at least break even. If your unit has been financed, however, your rental income will not be sufficient to offset your monthly payments, even with tax-deductible interest. But once you've paid off your loan, the financial picture will improve.

Bear in mind that you are still best advised to buy your interval unit to use. However, if you decide to rent out your time occasionally, you should expect to surpass your expenses.

A developer will probably be quite helpful to you if he still has units to sell, because you are not in competition with him, and your tenants could become his buyers. Like you, the renters would rather beat inflation than be part of it, and they are all too aware of the effects of inflation on yearly rentals.

The developer may provide rental assistance at a very low commission in order to encourage rentals and the resultant opportunity to develop new sales prospects. He may guide the resort in establishing the initial rental rates, since he has the most up-to-date information about competition and individual week value in the rental market place. You are not bound by these rates, but be careful not to price yourself out of the market. You can also lower your rates if the season is slow.

After the developer has sold all the units, he may stay with the resort under a management or service contract. Or your management may be an association, trust or several independent service organizations. Whichever is the case, evaluate their rental requests. You may want to use a backup agent in any case, if renting is really important to you.

Don't wait until the last minute! Plan far in advance and you'll be able to take steps if you're not happy with rental arrangements. If your vacation neighbors are aggressively marketing their rental weeks, you've got to do your homework and compete. Remember that families have a tendency to plan their vacations far in advance. They send away for brochures and make their final selection months ahead in order to make plans and often to benefit from transportation savings. Peak travel times often require reservations far in advance; if you control peak season weeks, keep this in mind when planning your strategy.

Does your organization belong to the local chamber of commerce or tourist board? These tourist centers receive volumes of requests for rental information and can be an excellent source for you and your resort. Naturally, your resort rental program should provide brochures and an enthusiastic staff, because they will be competing with all the other motels in the area.

You or your resort may establish a working arrangement with local brokers or agents. As with resales, brokers are trained to handle all areas of resort housing and will in all likelihood get excellent results for you. Again, you can set your own rental price as you see fit. If in time your unit has not been rented, lower your price. Even the lesser fee will help you in meeting that year's expenses.

Follow the same steps as outlined under resale procedures and you should be successful. Your company may be interested in renting your unit for one of their employees or a VIP client. Or, as many people do, you could simply make a grand gesture: let a relative use your weeks and be led to believe that you're rich!

CHAPTER 9

Your Legal Guidelines and Protection

In resort sharing, lawyers work with developers right from the beginning to insure that the developer operates well within state and local ordinances, and to assure as well that the consumer (you) will be fully protected under the law. It's simply good business for the developer to meet all the legal requirements at all levels.

The following pages describe the various government and industry watchdog organizations dedicated to protecting timesharing developers and consumers.

THE INDUSTRY ASSOCIATION

The National Timesharing Council (NTC) of the American Land Development Association (ALDA) is headquartered in Washington, D.C., and acts as a legislative voice and industry communicator to its 750 developer and marketer members. It apprises them of any changes in federal or state regulations concerning resort timesharing.

Recognizing their role of leadership in the industry,

153

NTC and ALDA have established a code of ethics, and they provide developers with a number of publications outlining acceptable standards. (You'll find a list of such publications at the end of this book.)

According to Jeanette Smith, director of communications for the association, ALDA devotes about half of its time to resort timesharing members. The rest of its work is involved with recreational lands, marketing efforts, land and laws. This independent nonprofit association expects its members to show complete integrity in the land and resort shelter business.

Not all ALDA members will abide by its code, so membership is not to be construed as a stamp of approval for a particular resort or developer. However, a member can be suspended or expelled from membership for noncompliance with the code.

ALDA holds at least 12 well-attended conferences or seminars on resort timesharing each year. At the informative sessions both members and observers of the industry share their experiences with an eye to improving resort standards, public relations and consumer protection.

Naturally, ALDA welcomes discussion from consumers about their assessment of the timesharing industry and its members. I have included ALDA's code of ethics for your information.

CODE OF ETHICS
AMERICAN LAND DEVELOPMENT ASSOCIATION

Preamble

The members of the American Land Development Association are dedicated to the principle of excellence in quality and service to provide the best possible environment for every American family.

They recognize land is a limited, basic natural resource and that its development is essential to the production, utilization, and increase of the nation's wealth. They are cognizant of their duty to conserve and maintain the land in their possession or under their control and ownership in a manner befitting a vital national resource.

They believe that the members of the land development industry, through free contractual relationships with the various land-consuming, land-utilizing, and land-conserving members of the public, can more perfectly create the means to bring about a balanced and efficient allocation of this limited resource. At the same time, they believe that traditional American private enterprise, functioning as it does in a diversified economy and under a democratic system of government, will most effectively achieve equity in distribution of land ownership and real property, along with a fair and equitable distribution of wealth and income produced therefrom.

In recognition of their interests and of their unique position to help achieve these high national goals, the members of the American Land Development Association subscribe to and dedicate themselves to promoting the following Code of Ethics.

1. Members shall make honesty and integrity the standard in all their commerce with consumers, whether representations are oral or written. They pledge to avoid misleading property descriptions, concealment of pertinent information, and exaggerations in advertising. They shall not market land for specific purposes if that land is not accessible and usable for such purposes.

2. Members shall make no false, misleading, or exaggerated claims with respect to the investment potential of the land.

3. Members shall endeavor to sell property only after the prospective purchaser has made an on-site inspection. In the event that no inspection is made, they shall be certain that the customer has received full and accurate disclosure through both visual and written materials describing the land being offered for sale.

They shall also offer the off-site buyer the option of rescinding his purchase within a specified time limit that is of sufficient duration to allow for and encourage inspection. They shall train their sales staff to observe this Code and to recognize the customer's interests.

4. Members shall consider it a duty to express financial and contractual obligations in written documents that comply with all applicable laws. They shall recognize that both full disclosure and clarity of disclosure are not only sound business practices, but also vital elements in achieving confidence among consumers.

5. Members shall not deny a person the right to purchase or lease any property or improvement because of race, color, creed, sex, religion, or national origin.

6. Members shall recognize the increasing importance of leisure time for the families in their developments and shall provide residents with means for recreation in the vicinity of their dwellings. They shall provide for those needs consistent with the master plan of the development. They shall also make suitable financial arrangements to assure completion of scheduled improvements.

7. Members shall design communities to foster continued owner involvement and civic pride. They shall form owner associations, where appropriate, to guarantee the continuation of sound policies. They shall establish deed covenants that will help protect the beauty of the land and the quality of life thereon.

8. Members pledge themselves to treat the land and the natural resources thereon with high purpose and with mature responsibility. They shall preserve the continuity of nature in advancing land designs which recognize the affinity between people and the land on which they live.

9. Members pledge themselves to preserve landmarks and structures of unique historic interest as well as to protect the natural vegetation and wildlife in a development to the greatest degree possible. The preservation areas are to be designated as such and held as open space with the necessary environmental controls to protect both natural and manmade resources from harm.

10. Members shall support all efforts to improve technology and methods of property development and to encourage research and development of new materials, concepts, and techniques.

11. Members shall endeavor to enlist all of the professional talents available to them in the fields of ecology, engineering, and architecture for the design of a development that strives for the best employment of the land and the protection of the environment. They shall endeavor to plan their developments with due consideration for open space and proper environmental controls.

12. Members shall plan, design, and build their developments in a manner consistent with public safety and health and comply with all laws, ordinances, and regulations applicable thereto.

13. Members shall keep apprised of all essential infor-

mation affecting the interests of the developers and of the public with respect to land, and shall support the industry in consultation with government authorities to insure legislation designed to improve the quality of land usage. They shall participate in idea-exchange programs with governmental agencies, boards, commissions, other associations, and consumers. Moreover, where governmental regulation is necessary, members shall contribute to adoption of effective and equitable statutes, regulations, and codes, shall abide by them, and shall cooperate in their enforcement by appropriate agencies and commissions.

14. Members shall conclude all business affairs with dignity and propriety. They shall avoid conflicts of interest and shall promote integrity as the highest ideal to be followed by all their employees.

15. Members shall be active supporters of the American Land Development Association's policies and shall not be content with passive contributions to the overall goals set forth by the organization.

16. Members shall immediately report any violation of this Code, whether their own or those of others, to the American Land Development Association Ethics Committee. Any deliberate or persistent departure from this Code of Ethics will result in appropriate disciplinary action, and may include expulsion from the American Land Development Association.

Conclusion

Members of the American Land Development Association must, above all, adhere to the highest ideals of moral conduct in their business relations. At no time shall an inducement of profit justify departure from this Code or from honorable business standards. When a member is faced with a unique situation, concerning which there is not provision in this Code of Ethics, he shall let the spirit of the Code guide him.*

Several states (as well as local municipalities) have passed legislation and local ordinances governing time-sharing in the interests of consumer protection and

---

* Reprinted by permission of the American Land Development Association.

proper disclosure and regulation. The National Time-sharing Council of the American Land Development Association is solidly behind such moves and the industry itself is complying with the various acts, regulations and bills to make certain that the industry is closed to unscrupulous developers and fast-buck artists.

ALDA and NTC committees have drafted what they feel is a model act and are asking the various states and communities to use that act as their guide in state and local regulation. It is called the NTC/NARELLO Act, and it endorses "disclosure" rather than "regulation," stating that the developer must disclose all that he is doing with the resort as must the vacation exchange groups.

The State of Nebraska was the first state to enact and pass a "timeshare act." Its purpose was to protect Nebraskans from "solicitations" of timeshared resorts anywhere unless the rules of disclosure are met.

THE MODEL TIMESHARE OWNERSHIP ACT

In the fall of 1979, two sponsoring organizations, the National Timesharing Council, the American Land Development Association and the National Association of Real Estate License Law Officials (NARELLO) adopted language for a proposed model timeshare act. They felt it to be of utmost importance both to the buying public and to the future of this relatively new industry to prescribe reasonable state regulation of timesharing. They especially wanted to avoid potential abuse and fraudulent sales practices. NARELLO is made up of representatives of state governments who are responsible for administering the real estate license laws in each of the fifty states.

In essence, the act would require any timeshare developer in any state to disclose all the pertinent facts about the development to a prospective buyer and then give that buyer a certain period of time in which to accept or terminate the transaction. The act addresses the "creation, termination and management" of the resort as well as offering protection to the purchasers.

The basic element of that protection is the public offering statement which must be given to each purchaser by the developer. Developers are required to hold in escrow all cash deposits until the mutual cancellation period has elapsed, and they must refund deposits immediately in the event of cancellation within the rescission period.

Developers must also report immediately to their buyers any change in the public offering statement as well as any liens, violations, criminal actions and matters that affect the buyers' ownership or right-to-use position. The act further requires registration of each development with the appropriate state agency, and that agency is given the power to investigate and regulate the actions of the developer and the development.

According to staff counsel for ALDA in Washington, most of the states currently considering such legislation are following the model act quite closely and are concentrating on disclosure bills rather than regulatory ones. Almost all are imposing criminal penalties for violations of the rules and some are varying the rescission periods from NTC/NARELLO's three days to seven and ten days as in Washington State and Florida, respectively. Washington State is concentrating on the matter through its securities laws while most other states are addressing the issue as a real estate matter.

Whatever the form of final action by the state, it is reassuring for you to know that the subject is being well covered and the industry itself is taking a leadership position in policing its own kinfolk.

GOVERNMENT REGULATIONS

The following information will clarify your position as an interval buyer under local, state and federal laws. Many of you may regard this as the "dry stuff" you always pass over in documents or books of this sort, but I urge you to read it carefully. I have done my best to translate legalese into more accessible language, and I think you will be convinced, if you had any lingering doubts, that timeshare developers are well regulated and buyers well protected under the law.

While no federal agencies are specifically responsible for the regulation of resort timesharing, numerous agencies administer laws, rules and guidelines which clearly affect how timesharing can be structured, marketed and sold.

There are three federal agencies whose role in timesharing is potentially significant: the Federal Trade Commission (FTC), the Department of Housing and Urban Development (HUD) and the Securities and Exchange Commission (SEC). Half a dozen other agencies may, at some time during the timeshare development process, become involved. These are the Federal Emergency Management Agency (federal flood insurance), Environmental Protection Agency (environmental controls on development), the Federal Home Loan Bank Board (regulations on savings and loan financing of timeshares), the Internal Revenue Service (tax regulations), the Federal Reserve Board (consumer credit and bank financing regulations) and the Department of Energy (through its expected Building Energy Performance Standards program).

The Federal Trade Commission

Currently, the FTC provides most of the federal consumer protection in the timesharing industry. Under Section 5 of the Federal Trade Commission Act, the agency is granted broad powers to regulate persons, companies and industries engaged in "unfair or deceptive acts and practices in or affecting commerce." Since the FTC first announced it was investigating the timesharing industry in 1975, it has continued to monitor timesharing by appearing at industry conferences and by actively responding to—and resolving—consumer complaints.

Commission staff members have worked with ALDA in settling complaints from timeshare buyers and have directly confronted timeshare developers with these complaints.

The FTC can take a variety of actions against companies believed to be engaging in unfair and deceptive practices. It can issue an administrative complaint which may result in years of litigation and adverse publicity; in these cases the developer may either sign a consent order which will bind him to certain remedial—and often onerous—actions specified by the FTC, or he may proceed through the entire litigation, which may result in a similar administrative or court order. The Commission may also sue a developer for civil penalties of up to $10,000 per violation of established rules or standards. Or the Commission may sue for consumer redress (rescission of contracts, refunds and damages).

However, existing FTC case law and trade regulation rules provide enough guidance for timesharing developers to avoid any major enforcement actions from this agency.

It is deceptive to:

1. Use a fictitious promotional plan or illusory contest as a device to obtain leads to prospective purchasers.

2. Represent that prospective customers are specially selected recipients of offers for vacations, goods or services, when such is not the case.

3. Represent that a particular product or service is being given away at no charge or that a bona fide contest is being conducted, when such is not the case.

4. Fail to affirmatively disclose material facts, such as the requirement that a participant attend a land sales presentation or pay a service charge, which would affect a consumer's decision to make a purchase of a vacation, goods or services.

5. Falsely represent that refunds are available or will be made where there is a failure or refusal to provide funds.

6. Falsely represent the true nature, character and activities of a business in order to induce the purchase of goods or services.

7. Falsely represent the existence of a relationship with, or connection to, any company, firm, or individual, including arrangements for cosponsorship or authority to act as a representative in order to induce the acceptance of an offer of a vacation, goods or services.

8. Represent that there is any limited time in which to accept the terms of an offer of a vacation, goods or services, when such is not the case.

9. Falsely represent the availability or quality of prizes or awards, including hotel/motel locations and accommodations.

10. Falsely represent the true cost, value or worth of the vacation, goods or services being offered.

11. Fail to affirmatively disclose that an offer of a vacation, goods or services is connected to the sale or promotion of any other goods or services, when such is the case.*

I hold several other practices to be unfair and deceptive in the land industry and think they should also be condemned by the timesharing industry:

1. Representing that timesharing is an entirely risk-free investment which can easily be resold at a profit.
2. Using adhesion contracts ("take it or leave it" contracts) which allow the seller to retain all payments made by the purchaser (regardless of actual damages suffered) upon the purchaser's default, without due consideration of mitigating circumstances.
3. Using high-pressure sales tactics.
4. Misrepresenting the availability of recreational facilities and amenities.
5. Failing to disclose material facts about the timeshare which would affect a consumer's decision to buy.

* Reprinted with permission

In addition to standards developed in FTC case law, two trade regulation rules apply to right-to-use timesharing (where no fee interest in real estate is conveyed). The first rule, Preservation of Consumer Claims and Defenses (Holder in Due Course Rule) [16 C.F.R. 433] requires that a specific notice be included in the installment sales contract. This notice allows the consumer to assert the same claims and defenses against a third-party holder of the contract as he can against the seller. The exact claims a consumer may bring vary according to state law. For example, if state law allows the consumer to cease paying on the contract because the seller fails to perform, the consumer can stop making payments to any lender holding the contract. The FTC staff believes right-to-use timesharing is a "novel form of consumer service." The rule applies only to goods and services, not interests in real estate.

The second rule, Cooling-Off Period for Door-to-Door Sales, also applies only to the sale of goods and services and thereby applies only to right-to-use timesharing. This rule requires that purchasers who sign sales contracts anywhere other than the seller's regular place of business (i.e., in the home, in a hotel room) be given a three-day rescission (cooling-off) right. The developer must give to each buyer a specified notice of cancellation outlining the procedures for cancelling and receiving a full refund.

Violation of either of these rules can subject the seller to fines of up to $10,000 for each violation.

The Federal Trade Commission also acts as the enforcement agency (with regard to nonfinancial institution creditors) for two other laws which timeshare developers must consider: the Truth-in-Lending Act and its implementing Regulation Z, and the Equal Credit Opportunity Act, Regulation B. The Truth-in-Lending Act requires that certain specific disclosures be given to consumers when they finance a purchase. In addition, Regulation Z spells out how credit terms can be advertised. This law and regulation apply to all timeshare developers who offer financing to their purchasers.

Department of Housing and Urban Development

HUD administers two laws applicable to resort time-sharing. The Fair Housing Law (Title VIII of the Civil Rights Act of 1968) prohibits discrimination in the sale, rental, advertising and financing of housing on the basis of race, color, religion, sex or national origin. Individual complaints of discrimination to HUD are generally settled through negotiation (voluntary compliance) and consent orders. However, where there appears to be a pattern or practice of discrimination, complaints are referred to the Department of Justice's Civil Rights Division for prosecution.

The Interstate Land Sales Full Disclosure Act, administered by the Office of Interstate Land Sales Registration (OILSR) at HUD, can also apply to timesharing. However, most timeshare developers should be completely exempt from the act. The act does not apply to the sale of lots on which there is a "residential, commercial, condominium or industrial building, or the sale or lease of land under a contract obligating the seller or lessor to erect such a building within a period of two years" [15 U.S.C. 1702(a) (2)]. Developers selling timeshares in completed buildings or who unconditionally obligate themselves in the sales contract to erect the building or unit within two years from the date of sale are clearly exempt from this act.

Securities and Exchange Commission

The SEC has potential jurisdiction over any form of resort timesharing which would fall within the definition of "security" as it appears in the Securities Act of 1933 and the Exchange Act of 1934, or as it has been interpreted by the courts. In the early 1970s, the SEC issued a release describing the conditions under which the sale of a condominium would constitute the sale of the security: primarily when the condominium included a rental pooling arrangement or other profit-sharing agreement. With regard to timesharing, however, the SEC is silent. During the mid-1970s, new timeshare developers requested and obtained from the Commission staff "no action" letters which at least stated that no enforcement action would be taken if the timeshares were sold without SEC registration. Near the end of the decade, the Commission had directed its staff to issue no opinions or interpretations on whether or not a particular timeshare offering could be a security. Thus, developers must now rely on opinions of private counsel.

If the offering of timeshare to consumers were to be held as a security, it would be because the offering fell under the definition of "investment contract," as that term has been interpreted in the courts. Briefly, an investment contract can often be established where (1) a person invests money in an enterprise (2) for which he expects to receive profits and (3) the enterprise has established the possibility of profits (4) based on the efforts of third parties (5) over which the investor has no effective control. However, the Supreme Court in *U.H.F.* v. *Foreman* [421 U.S. 837 (1975)] stated ". . . when a purchaser is motivated by a desire to use or consume the item purchased—'to occupy the land or to develop it themselves'. . . the security laws do not apply."

Therefore, timeshare programs which avoid using any investment sales pitch, place ultimate control of management of the resort in the owners/members, stress that purchase should be made for personal use and enjoyment of the buyer and, in some cases, even prohibit resale of the timeshare at a profit, can probably be exempt from regulation under the federal securities laws. State securities laws also can have local jurisdiction and different viewpoints.

ARE LAWYERS AND ACCOUNTANTS HELPFUL?

Many attorneys and accountants may be as unfamiliar as you are with the timesharing concept. If you are going to rely on an accountant or attorney for advice on your purchase, be sure he knows all the intricacies of time-sharing.

While on vacation you may find a resort you really like at a price that makes sense. What happens when you take the paperwork back home and show it to an attorney? If he is new to the concept, he may not show much enthusiasm for it. Prevail upon him to call the resort or attorney who drew up the documents to discuss the matter. Before you accept his advice, you'd like to feel he has a good understanding of timesharing.

In an attempt to educate American lawyers, the resort sharing industry established a counsel of attorneys who will in turn disseminate information to other attorneys who may ultimately be helpful to you.

Or you may prefer this approach: rather than simply asking for a judgment from an attorney or accountant, start with specific questions regarding those areas you do not understand or on which you think you'll need special protection.

In areas where there are many interval resorts, you will be more likely to find an attorney or accountant cognizant of the details of the industry and consequently more capable of helping you with specific questions.

Sensible developers will not state that resort timesharing is sold as an investment opportunity unless they are registered with the SEC, because such assertions would otherwise be in violation of the securities regulations. However, purchasers can make up their own minds about prime-time investments and buy for rental or future resale income.

OTHER LEGAL GUARDIANS

More closely located and attuned to your needs are two somewhat interrelated groups—your owners' association and your exchange network.

The owners' association, because of its interest in protecting the resort and property, also becomes a protection for each owner. Should an owner need legal redress that would affect the majority of other owners, the association has the authority and ability to retain counsel and take appropriate action. This does not mean that the association will take sides on private matters or issues involving internal owner differences, unless those items are of concern to the integrity and quality of the resort. In fact, an owner who disregards the association's rules and regulations or is in default of fees can find himself on the receiving end of legal action.

The exchange network will not go to bat legally for its members, but it will react on declining quality standards at its member resorts on behalf of resort members or owners. Complaints to the exchange network, either from buyers or exchangers, provide the network with an incentive to investigate major problems so that effective service will still be maintained for those wanting to trade in or out of the resort. Continued abuses of set standards can lead to expulsion or cessation of trading until corrective action takes place.

Understanding that the networks are very important to their members, developers and resort management have been very responsive to regular reviews by the networks, and drastic measures have rarely been indicated.

CHAPTER 10

What Is the Future of Timesharing?

According to *Resort Timesharing Today* publisher, Carl Burlingame, at the turn of a new decade:

> Nineteen eighty was a *very* good year. In fact, the industry's remarkable continued growth may have caused some developers to rub their eyes in astonishment, especially those who survived the mid-70s struggle in real estate. Despite 20%-plus peaks in the prime interest rate, and in a limping general economy, U.S. interval sales broke vigorously through the billion-a-year level and are still charting a steep upward curve.

In 1980 a record number of projects got underway in California and Florida. In 1981 the rate of new entrants remained high, although tight money and new regulatory restraints in a number of states restricted full growth potential.

Burlingame stated,

> During 1980, at least 18 developers had sales of $10 million or more, almost double the number of firms in this

class last year. And these larger companies alone booked a whopping one-third of a *billion* dollars in sales. The ranks of $10 million-plus firms will probably double again during 1981, judging by the outlook for the sizeable number of companies that did $5–$10 million last year.

Resort sharing's explosive 1980 growth was mirrored in the fact that the industry's sales leaders booked 79 percent more in sales than the previous year. According to Burlingame,

> Most of these leaders were multi-location operations, and four of the five highest-volume firms were club-type programs offering their own exchange system. In fact, three of the five—AIV, the Aloha Group, and Sweetwater —reached a size verging on self-sufficiency so far as exchange is concerned, with all three relying far less than before on their outside exchange service, RCI or I.I. for trades.

NEW IDEAS AND PRODUCTS

Not only is resort sharing catching on worldwide, but as with any innovative idea, it is maturing and changing as it grows. In the future you're likely to see the concept applied to most types of vacations. Campgrounds are being timeshared on both an ownership and membership basis. We've already seen resort sharing plans that aren't even on land—boats, for example—and we're likely to see quite a few more. Vacationers can purchase a week on a luxurious sailboat that skims over the waters of the Caribbean and serves up gourmet meals to its passengers under the stars. And if you are a serious fisherman, instead of chartering a boat by the day or week, why not own or share it at a fraction of the full cost?

Because of the popularity of the concept and the still largely untapped sales potential of 31 million North American families, many believe that resorts may someday specialize and become what one leader calls "affinity resorts," catering to prospective owners who enjoy a specific recreation atmosphere as their primary entertainment. Just as there are week-long golf and tennis packages today at "normal" motels and hotels, there may be similar resort-shared developments in the next few years. Consider, also, the dude ranches and fitness farms that are popping up all over the country and apply to them the concept of resort sharing.

A Florida stable which offers lessons and riding by the hour to the "horsey" set now "intervals" its animals. One horse is then "owned" by as many as 30 families who share in the housing and feeding of the animal as well as their riding time.

Many observers of the leisure industry feel labor unions may soon ask for vacation facilities in their contracts, in addition to paid vacations, requesting the employer to defray certain costs of vacation accommodations.

As the resort sharing industry expands and an influx of new resorts floods the market, the sales of resort unit weeks will become attractive to the highly computerized real estate companies now in business, and mass marketing will further accelerate the sales volume.

Because on-site competition is becoming too costly in many resort areas, the off-site trend will most likely expand in the future, bringing forth thousands of new off-site brokers to handle the increasing number of projects.

An exciting trend to look for, too, is that of urban resort sharing. Resorts were already established in Waikiki and Las Vegas; some of 1980s entrants were in San Francisco, New Orleans and other urban areas. Because these cities are vacation resorts and host large numbers of tourists, it is logical that they would appear on the interval scene. Industry developers are considering still another marketing dimension to interval resorts in populous cities— those to be purchased by suburbanites to enjoy the city's attractions, or those used by corporations, as lodging for visiting executives and as rewards for top producers. For example, in a new experiment with urban timesharing in San Francisco, owners of Powell Place, a prestigious Nob Hill development, don't have to use their seven days all at once, as most projects require. They may also trade shares for time at other resorts through RCI.

As the resort sharing industry matures, the peripheral services required to meet the need for its smooth operation are beginning to emerge. New businesses and careers are being established to fulfill these needs. The exchange networks were the first. They are being followed by resort management services, public relations specialists on resort sharing, credit companies to finance unit sales and developers who are franchising their resort systems.

As the industry grows and matures, consumers are going to benefit. The new franchise operations are a good example. An experienced and successful resort-share development company is only going to lend its name to operations of similar quality. And, while you're not likely to see a resort on every corner, franchise operations are making it easier for builders and resort operators alike to get their developments off the ground with less problems than if they had been on their own. Thus, as major developers begin to systematize their operations, standards within the industry should become even better. These companies will be setting their own high standards and will be able to assure prospective buyers that resorts bearing their name will be of superior value. With the advent of national and, eventually, international franchise operations, vacation choices for quality-conscious consumers will be greatly enhanced.

Whatever direction resort sharing ultimately takes, this newest development in real estate will continue to offer vacationers all the benefits of an expensive second home without the burden of paying for the whole thing. What's more, it will also provide a chance to do something about ever-present inflation which might otherwise affect the quantity and quality of family vacations.

STABILIZATION OF THE GROWTH CURVE

Of major importance to the interval resort industry is the promise of more and more leisure time for jobholders in the coming years. From long holiday weekends to more paid vacation time, more families than ever before will want to participate in the interval concept. I think that once they learn the basics they will really enjoy their slice of the vacation pie.

So you can see that the industry has enjoyed phenomenal growth since its real emergence in 1975, and I'm very optimistic about where it will go from here, too.

The Ragatz survey (see page 179) indicates that most of the first wave of buyers earned above-average incomes and were therefore more able to take risks on a new venture. Now thousands of people with more modest incomes have begun to follow their lead.

"Too good to be true" has been the byword for those who doubted the viability of interval resort sharing. Enough statistics have been compiled to prove that what once seemed too good is now also true. People like to vacation. And despite double-digit inflation and soaring interest rates, interval resort sharing makes it possible for people to vacation. Even if you had left the money you paid for your interval unit in the bank, you'd still be faced with laying out more cash each year for that hard-earned vacation.

The interval industry is also subject to inflation, of course, and some of its spiraling costs will have to be passed on to newcomers. Acquisition costs for prime vacation property are soaring. Construction costs are keeping pace with inflation. So are the costs of labor, utilities and furnishings. All the ingredients for a nice vacation resort will be reflected in future prices. Interval prices today are not as low as they were five years ago.

Developers are concerned about the possibility of decline in the quantity and quality of interval resorts in the face of inflation, but they will find a way to maintain standards as long as the buyers come forth.

Local legislation is not always sympathetic to interval resorts, either. In contrast to the in-season boom enjoyed by shops and restaurants in tourist areas whose businesses then become more stabilized in the off season, interval resort sharing provides a continuous flow of tourists. Community governments are worried about destruction of the community infrastructure and increased demand on utilities and natural resources. Strict zoning laws have resulted in elimination of interval resorts in places like Lake Tahoe, Nevada, and some of the coastlines of Florida, Massachusetts and California.

But developers appreciate the concerns of community groups, and are working hard to see that communities are not adversely affected. It is as much in the developers' interests as that of the communities to see that the resort areas remain attractive, well kept and financially stable.

WHERE WILL THE BANKS STAND?

Developers don't usually provide financing for their customers, and that is especially true today with building costs so high. Most buyers will have to arrange outside financing.

In the past, only local banks agreed to help their developers by arranging mortgages for their consumers. Fortunately for both developers and consumers, lending institutions have realized that loans for interval purchases provide excellent short-term revenue, because the mortgages are backed either by real estate equity or by a personal loan guarantee.

The quantum leaps of the industry have outstripped the lenders' commitments to some degree, but more and more financial institutions all over the world are now investigating this industry. One of the largest timeshare lenders, San Diego-based Security Pacific Finance (a subsidiary of Pacific National Bank, which is ranked in the top ten in the U.S.), had over $70 million committed to timeshare loans at the close of 1980; no limit has been set for future expansion, but the growth of the industry is now entering a phase in which it will need over *one billion dollars a year* in commitments to meet the financing demand.

Some large institutions like Citibank and Mellon became involved in 1980, making significant construction and takeout loans. Federally chartered savings and loan associations and mutual banks can now make timeshare loans as a result of regulations adopted by the Federal Home Loan Bank Board in late 1980. Most observers think savings and loan companies will continue to move cautiously in implementing their new authority to participate; others feel that the shorter-term and solid-yield timeshare potential will hasten their involvement. The preamble to their new guidelines relates that any of the various kinds of timesharing, whether of an ownership or right-to-use form, may be financed as a consumer loan.

We still have to face the forecast for tough economic conditions in the future. In real estate, it is still a sellers' market, although prices and terms for buyers are looking better all the time. Even some of the most conservative economists are coming out in favor of resort timesharing and believe it's possible to make meaningful projections on its growth. They see that resort sharing is a new product created as a response to unsettling conditions, one of them high inflation. It is not an old product being squeezed by inflation as, say, the automobile has been. The big car was essentially created by 35¢-per-gallon gasoline. High fuel costs then made small cars the norm, and the effect on Detroit has been disquieting because small cars are less profitable.

Resort timesharing, by contrast, is an industry on the move because its purpose is to combat inflation; for now, a smaller piece of the pie is the only way to go.

THE CORPORATE MARKET

One of the last bastions for the interval industry to confront is the corporate market. Interestingly, surveys show that initial buyers of resort timesharing were professionals, yet the incidence of these executives carrying their personal experiences over into their business has been noticeably rare. Some small- and medium-size companies have recognized the opportunities resort sharing provides, but most of the major companies are still untapped, although most companies could make considerable use of a block of units at a resort!

Recent estimates regarding credit card usage for lodging and meals indicated that a whopping 80 percent of the charges were incurred by executives traveling on behalf of their companies. Urban resort sharing for the corporate market could save companies tens of thousands of accommodation dollars, and the exchange networks could add variety and flexibility.

Major companies spend small fortunes on employee incentives and are always looking for something more exciting and dramatic. How about winning a week's vacation in your choice of Las Vegas, Vail, New Orleans, San Francisco or Hilton Head? Or a week in London and a week in the Alps? Or vacations for a lifetime in Florida or Hawaii or New Hampshire as an incentive for the most productive employees?

Ingenuity and imagination have been the bulwark of American business. It would seem that part of the growth of the interval resort industry will come from the awakening giants all around us.

CHAPTER 11

Who Are the People Involved?

Before exploring who the people are who actually occupy timesharing units and learning what the media have to say, we should pause for a moment to comment on the developers themselves and the costs they incur in launching a timesharing development.

The early days of resort timesharing were marked by some growing pains and, here and there, a little negative publicity. A few resorts floundered, others were guilty of high-pressure land sales tactics, still others were simply below acceptable standards.

The media was skeptical about timesharing at that point, too, but their views have changed considerably, as you'll see at the end of this chapter.

One early misconception about interval resorts concerned the financial aspects—developers were accused of taking excessive profits. While this notion has been largely dispelled, you might like to have some clarification of the financial picture from the developer's point of view. There is no question, of course, that an interval

177

resort developer brings in significantly more money from a 40-unit development than he would if he were simply selling the units outright. However, his overhead is tremendously higher than that of the condominium developer, and as a result the profit margin remains quite similar to that in other types of real estate.

The interval resort developer has to furnish and equip all 40 units—plus a model—right down to the corkscrew. Because of the heavy use of units, everything must be of the very best quality, as well as provide the elegance promised to prospective buyers. He must launch a huge marketing campaign, for he is not looking for just 40 buyers, he is looking for 40 buyers for 51 weeks of the year. The cost of promotion—brochures, postage, and radio, TV, and newspaper/magazine ads—to reach a projected 10,000 "lookers" is staggering. Not to mention the staff to handle the marketing and sales. Operational and administrative costs are onerous as well, and the time and expense required to prepare over 1,000 deeds, title insurance policies and other legal documents further add to his financial burden. Naturally, he will make some money; he isn't in the business just to meet new people. But in the end his profits will be reasonable, and buyers need not worry about ripoffs.

WHO WILL YOUR NEIGHBORS BE?

Understanding the need to move from guestimates into more concrete facts, the National Timesharing Council (industry association and division of the American Land Development Association, known as ALDA) organized an in-depth questionnaire to be used in 1979 to compile current and valid data on buyers' attitudes to resort timesharing.

Utilizing the independent research firm of Richard L. Ragatz Associates of Eugene, Oregon, 20,730 questionnaires were mailed to timeshare buyers of 33 participating resorts located in the U.S. Another 6,000 were mailed to a sampling of members in the two exchange networks.

The response rate was very good. Industry experts estimate there were 215,000 timeshare families in the U.S. when the survey was completed in the spring of 1980. The high rate of return, when utilizing the statistical sampling theory coupled with the sizable representation of the interval population, gives credence to the reliability of projecting the survey results to encompass the entire U.S. timeshare public.

According to Dick Ragatz, who compiled all the answers to the 75 questions, the typical timeshare purchaser was 45, married, had a college degree and had a family income of $33,500. "These solidly Middle-American demographics (relative affluence, middle age, and upscale educational attainment) indicate the market is composed of a stable population fairly well insulated from extreme impact of a recession."

The study also revealed that these buyers are exceptionally well satisfied with their interval purchases, with nearly two-thirds planning to buy additional time. A significant portion of future interval sales could well be repeat customers satisfied with their initial exposure.

Over 50% of respondents had 1979 household incomes of $30,000 or more; and 17% were in the $50,000-plus bracket. The median income—$33,500—was more than twice the 1979 median income ($16,500) for all U.S. households.

From an age standpoint, timeshare buyers are squarely within the prime U.S. market for goods and services with over one-half the household heads between the ages of 34 and 54 and the vast majority (89%) married couples.

... One of the most striking findings is the extraordinary high level of educational attainment of respondents. Three out of four attended college, over half are college graduates, and nearly one-third did graduate-level work. This would indicate a high level of professionals (attorneys, CPAs, doctors, etc.) among timeshare owners.

Buyers very satisfied

(percent of buyers, adds to 100%)

Very satisfied	44%
Satisfied	42%
So-so	9%
Dissatisfied	3%
Very dissatisfied	2%

Upscale incomes

(percent of buyers, adds to 100%)

$50,000+	17%
$40,000–$49,999	15%
$30,000–$39,999	24%
$20,000–$29,999	29%
under $20,000	15%

Note: Median income - $33,500.

Well-educated

(percent of household/heads, adds to 100%)

Graduate level work	31%
College degree	24%
Some college	21%
H.S. diploma	21%
Less than 11 years	3%

Note: Median education level - 15.4 years (college degree-plus)

Satisfied with exchange

(percent of buyers who had traded, adds to 100%)

Very satisfied	53%
Satisfied	37%
Dissatisfied	10%

Why they bought

(percent of buyers, does not add to 100%)*

Exchange opportunity	71%
Save money on vacation	59%
Investment potential	39%
Liked unit	30%
Liked rec facilities	29%
Certainty of accommodations	24%
Own 2nd home at low cost	23%
Other	4%

*Respondents could check more than one answer.

2/3 to buy more

(percent of buyers, does not add to 100%)

Buy more time at present resort	25%
Buy more time at other resort	37%
Buy no more time	40%
Buy no more, sell present time	19%

*Respondents could check more than one answer.

Most in 35-54 age group

(percent of household/heads, adds to 100%)

Under 25	3%
25–34	19%
35–44	22%
45–54	31%
55–64	20%
64+	5%

Note: Median age - 45.

By a significant margin, the top purchase motivations were: (1) saving money on future vacation costs and (2) exchange opportunities (a 1978 study also put these two reasons at the top of the list). Since both these motives relate to vacationing interests rather than to real estate values, it seems clear that buyers perceive timesharing primarily as a vacation plan. But there was considerable interest in real estate values (especially by fee programs

buyers), as resale potential ranks as the third-highest mo-
tivational impetus.

According to the survey, 60 percent own at resorts
within an approximate five-hour drive (250 miles) of
their primary residence and 50 percent within a three-
hour drive (150 miles). Thus, a majority of timeshare
owners are not affected by energy-related rising airfare
costs, except when and if they trade to a more distant
resort. At the same time, 40 percent own intervals at resorts over 250 miles from their home and 26 percent own
at resorts 1,000 miles or more from home: these owners
tended to have higher incomes.

"Obviously the high level of buyer satisfaction—nearly
90% of respondents are satisfied or very satisfied with
their purchase—bodes well for the industry. It indicates
that timesharing is gathering a wave of public acceptance
and favorable word-of-mouth advertising from the experiences of satisfied buyers."

Two-thirds of the buyers in the survey planned to purchase more intervals either at their present resort (25 percent) or at another resort (37 percent). The average
amount of annual time owned is 1.8 weeks, even though
most buyers have more than 1.8 weeks of vacation time
each year.

Of respondents who had used their exchange service
(37 percent), 90 percent of these said their trading experience was satisfactory or very satisfactory. A high level of
future trading activity is anticipated, since 50 percent
indicated they plan to exchange every year or two.

Although areas of dissatisfaction were relatively small,
they merit attention. There was a dissatisfaction about
shopping facilities, restaurants and recreation for children as well as facility management and cleanliness of
the unit. With exchanges, 10.4 percent indicated an un-
satisfactory experience and 14.3 percent complained that
the exchange had not been fairly represented (the two
findings may be related).

Finally, 12.4 percent said in hindsight they would not

have purchased, and 18.6 percent said they planned to sell their interval and would not buy more time.

High satisfaction, according to Ragatz, was most apparent among respondents who (1) owned their timeshare longer and had used it more, (2) purchased more than one week, (3) bought higher-priced intervals in larger units (4) purchased for use and were very satisfied with their unit, (5) had a very satisfactory trading experience and felt exchange had been fairly represented, (6) were middle-aged, and above all, (7) had more education and high incomes.

The respondents lived in 47 states with only Mississippi, North Dakota and South Dakota not represented. Over one-half (52.2 percent) of the respondents owned their timeshares in just two states (Florida and Pennsylvania). In regard to location of primary homes, over half (54.9 percent) live in the five states of California, Florida, Michigan, New Jersey and Pennsylvania.

Compared to the huge numbers of vacationing middle-income North Americans who could be timeshare owners, the industry has barely scratched the surface of the potential market. Although originally devised for the average-income family, half of all timeshare owners had family incomes over $33,500 in 1979. The next group of buyers will undoubtedly come from lower-income levels as the viability of the concept is enhanced by good publicity and satisfied owners.

WHAT THE MEDIA HAS TO SAY

Happily, as more interval ownership developments have been built and sold, both the public and the press have become aware of the great benefits resort sharing has to offer. Articles hailing individual ownership as the wave of the future abound in well-respected magazines and newspapers. In fact, there is hardly a major U.S. or Canadian publication that has not run an article on the industry. Here is what some of them have to say:

From *Money* (America's foremost consumer finance publication)—3/20/80:

> Time shares can provide buyers with the amenities of a vacation home without high mortgage payments and year-around maintenance hassles.

From *House Beautiful* (a leading publication in the field of home furnishings and design)—10/79:

> The time-sharing plan is the hottest new real estate phenomenon in America since the condominium was unveiled in the early 1950s. It permits anyone—everyone—to buy several weeks per year at a vacation home for only a few thousand dollars. It permits you to buy forty years of future vacations at 1979 prices to earn a 10 to 12 percent return on your investment, to buy only as much vacation as you want and to use your two to three bedrooms to hold family and friends at no charge. It also permits you, through a houseswapping service, to stay at more than 200 resorts around the world—for just $36 per year.

From *Business Week*—6/4/79:

> It's a dandy hedge against escalating rental rates and far less expensive than buying a second home.

From *Barron's Business & Financial Weekly* (one of this country's most prestigious financial publications)—11/26/79:

> Whatever the particular form, it looks as though interval ownership is the vacation product of the future. It offers consumers the unlikely combination of luxury and affordability and gives prudent developers an opportunity to vastly improve profit potential.

From *MacLean's* (the largest weekly newsmagazine in Canada)—3/10/80:

> In Canada, where a fledgling half-dozen projects had sales of about $20 million in 1979, 12 to 15 new projects are

already on the books for 1980–81 and Canadian sales are projected to reach $100 million within three years. With no tropical beaches to seduce would-be weekly squatters, most of Canada's time capsules are clustered in the Rockies and Laurentians to attract skiers.

From *Apartment Life*—6/79 (with reference to exchange opportunities):

Inflation-proof vacations . . . time-sharing locks in the price, not where you go.

From *Prime Time*—1/80:

In 300 resorts from Florida to Hawaii—and in dozens more located in Europe, Mexico, the Caribbean, Central America, South America, Canada, Australia and the Middle East—tens of thousands of converted skeptics are buying time shares. Estimated U.S. sales leapt from $25 million in 1975 to $700 million in 1979, and real estate developers, heartbeats quickening, anticipate geometrically higher figures in the near future.

From *Changing Times*, The Kiplinger Magazine—1/78:

. . . time-sharing may be just what you've been looking for. . . . it brings [expensive resort condos] within reach.

From *Leisure*—3/24/78:

You can have "your" place at the mountains or the beach and access to all those exotic world resorts for about the price of a new car. . . .

From *Travel & Leisure*—6/77:

A time-share project offers a built-in hedge against inflation.

From *The Miami Herald*—11/13/77:

. . . it's one of the hottest vacation ideas on the market today.

Glossary

Amenities: Parts of the common areas as well as certain items in the dwelling unit that are there for beauty, pleasure and fun, i.e., swimming pool, tennis courts, bikes, landscaping, etc.

Annual Percentage Rate (APR): The actual cost of the money borrowed on a purchase, expressed as a percentage per annum.

Budget: The schedule of the actual costs of operating and maintaining a resort, usually based on estimates of expenditures for a specific period of time.

Closing: The actual completion of the transaction acknowledging satisfaction of all legal and financial obligations between buyer and seller; recording of the deed and disbursement of funds to appropriate channels is the final step in closing.

Closing Costs: Such items as legal fees, documentary stamps, title insurance premiums, service charges, etc., which are due at the time of the sale.

Club Plan: A form of right-to-use in which a member may purchase the right to use a condominium, although not a specific one, for a prescribed length of time. Members simply belong to and do not own the resort.

Common Areas: The areas of the development that are outside the actual dwelling unit, such as swimming pools or tennis courts, that are owned and used by all owners or members.

Condominium Association: A group, created by a formal charter and composed of all of the owners of a condominium, which attends to the affairs of the resort.

Condominium Association Board of Directors: A smaller group, elected by members of the association, that elects the association's officers to maintain day-to-day control over the resort.

Condominium Declaration ("condo docs"): An extensive set of legal documents establishing a property as a con-

185

dominium, defining the parameters and specifically listing the ingredients of ownership.

Conversion: The changing of a structure from some other use such as an apartment, condominium, hotel or motel to use as a resort timesharing development.

Deed: Usually a general warranty deed conveying title certificating ownership of a fee-simple unit week from developer to customer.

Developer: The entity that creates, builds, sells, converts or otherwise brings the resort into being.

Disclosure Statement: Details of the purchase and a breakdown of the costs and distribution of funds at the closing.

Down Payment: That amount of cash required on a contract where the major portion of the cost is to be financed.

Estate: The title or interest one has in property such as real estate and personal property that can, if desired, be passed on to survivors at the time of one's death.

Exchange Program: A program offering resort timesharing buyers the option of trading their unit weeks for the same weeks at another resort, in many worldwide locations; it also offers the opportunity to exchange unit weeks for different unit weeks, either at the same resort or at other worldwide locations.

Fee-Simple: A manner of owning land, in one's own name, free of any condition, limitations or restrictions.

I.I.: Interval International. An organization established to handle exchanges, located in Miami, Florida.

Interval Ownership: Actual ownership with deed and title insurance; the owner can use the property, rent it, loan it, or will it in his or her estate. One owns just the amount of time one can pleasurably use, and pays maintenance only for the time owned, not for the entire year.

Lease: A form of right-to-use in which one simply leases, rather than buys, the right to use a particular unit for a period of time, usually 20 to 30 years. The lease is bought at the current market price, but the unit is never owned.

Maintenance Fee: The annual fee assessed to owners to cover the costs of maintenance and management of the resort, for only the amount of time they purchased.

Management Agreement: A contract between the owner(s) and a management team to handle the actual day-to-day operations and maintenance of the resort.

Mini-Vacation: A short stay at a resort, perhaps one night and two days, to give the prospective buyer an opportunity to examine the resort and make a buying decision.

Non-disturbance: A protective clause or inclusion in the sales agreement assuring the purchaser occupancy of his timeshare interval regardless of default by the developer or owner(s) of the resort.

Per Diem: Occupancy, maintenance and service costs incurred by owner, over and above base maintenance charges, when owner's unit is occupied. Not used at all resorts.

Prospectus: The display, required of all developers, of the information pertinent to the purchase and to the resort itself. A booklet of disclosures about every facet of the purchase.

Purchase Contract: The actual agreement to buy and sell or to lease the time and space in the resort, involving two or more individuals, whereby each becomes obligated to the other, with reciprocal rights to demand performance of what is promised by each respectively.

RCI: Resort Condominiums International. An organization established to handle exchanges, located in Indianapolis, Indiana.

Resale Program: Usually a division established by the developer or some other real estate broker to handle the resale of unit weeks or leaseholds should an owner wish to divest his interest in the property.

Rescission: That period of time following the sale during which the buyer can change his mind, cancel the purchase agreement and get a refund of funds paid on deposit. It varies from state to state from three to 15 days.

Right-to-Use: An alternative to ownership where the developer of a property retains ownership and the customer is only given the contractual right to use and enjoy a certain property or place for a specified period of time.

Title Insurance: An insurance policy written by a highly specialized company that agrees to defend the status of the title to the unit week(s).

Tour: The sales trip through the sales offices, model apartments and the amenities by which the salesperson familiarizes the prospective buyer with the property.

Unit Week: That specific increment of time and physical space that makes up the actual purchase of vacation time in a fee-simple project.

Key Regulatory and Industry Organizations

Several major organizations and ancillary entities have helped bring resort timesharing to its present popularity in an amazingly short period of time. For the benefit of the consumer who may wish to contact them for additional information, they have been listed below. Most of them have been discussed in this book.

Canadian Timesharing Council
Suite 1903
P.O. Box 12
Toronto Dominion Center
Toronto, Ontario M5K 1A8

Federal Trade Commission
FTC Building
Room 264
Washington, D.C. 20508

Interval International
7000 S.W. 62nd Avenue
Suite 306
South Miami, FL 33143

National Timesharing Council of the American Land
   Development Association
1000 16th Street, N.W.
Suite 604
Washington, D.C. 20036

Resort Condominiums International
P.O. Box 80229
Indianapolis, IND 46204

The Time Sharing Institute
P.O. Box 4301920
South Miami, FL 33143

Typical Resort Maintenance Budget

MOTEL CONVERSION
27 units—1 bedroom, 1 bath
800-square-feet apartments

	1981
Revenue	
Maintenance	$ 75,735.00
Per diem—est.	57,834.00
Interest income	-0-
Other income	-0-
Total Revenue	$133,569.00
Expenses	
Accounting and legal	$ 2,400.00
Association meetings	1,200.00
Books, magazines and newspapers	5,263.00
Unit supplies	2,885.00
Electricity—unit	16,000.00
Gas—pool and barbeque	3,000.00
Insurance	3,600.00
License—occupational	150.00
Maintenance—lawn	150.00
Maintenance—bldg. and equip., pool, rec.	6,500.00
Maintenance—weeks	5,400.00
Management fee	13,800.00
Office and postage	2,962.00
Payroll and taxes	29,327.00
Pest control	452.00
Reserve for depreciation	6,900.00
Reserve for maintenance	6,900.00
Telephone	1,200
Unit cleaning	18,655.00
Waste disposal	1,594.00
Water and sewer	4,131.00
Maintenance—elevator	1,100.00
Total Expense	$133,569.00

Bibliography

For readers wishing to pursue timesharing further, we recommend the following publications.

Bloch, Stuart Marshall, and William B. Ingersoll, Eds., *Timesharing*. The Urban Land Institute, 1200 18th Street, N.W., Washington, D.C. 20036, 1977.

Burlingame, Carl H., Ed., *Buyer's Guide to Resort Timesharing*. The CHB Co., Inc., P.O. Box 184, Los Altos, California 94022, 1977.

Burlingame, Carl H., Ed., *Directory of Resort & Recreational Development*. The CHB Co., Inc., P.O. Box 184, Los Altos, California 94022, 1977.

Burlingame, Carl H., Ed., *Resort Timesharing TODAY*. The CHB Co., Inc., P.O. Box 184, Los Altos, California 94022. Published twice monthly.

Burlingame, Carl H., and Dr. Richard L. Ragatz, *Timeshare Purchasers, Who They Are, Why They Buy*. The CHB Co., Inc., P.O. Box 184, Los Altos, California 94022, spring 1981.

Davis, Thomas J., and Mario F. Rodriguez, *Marketing a Time Sharing Project*. Time Sharing Institute, Box 4301920, South Miami, Florida 33143, 1977.

Davis, Thomas J., and Mario F. Rodriguez, *Structuring the Interval Project—From Conception to Marketing*. Time Sharing Institute, 7000 S.W. 62nd Avenue, South Miami, Florida 33143, 1975.

Ingersoll, William B., Stuart Marshall Bloch, and Stephany A. Masden, Eds., *Digest of State Land Sales Regulations*. Land Development Institute, Ltd., 1404 16th Street, N.W., Washington, D.C. 20036, 1977.

National Timesharing Council of the American Land Development Association, Pub., *Resort Timesharing, a Consumer's Guide*. ALDA, Suite 604, Solar Building, 1000 16th Street, N.W., Washington, D.C. 20036, 1977.

Romney, Keith, *A Timesharing Guide*. Keith Romney and Associates, 134 S. Main Street, Salt Lake City, Utah 84101, 1980.

Acknowledgments

Because there has been so little written about timesharing, most of our research depended on interviews with a wide variety of people in the resort sharing industry. Most of them are specialists in certain facets of the business.

I am especially grateful to attorneys Stuart Bloch and William Ingersoll; Interval International's Mario Rodriguez and Tom Davis; the Time Sharing Institute's Wayne Schiefelbeim; Jon De Haan and Carol Trexler of Resort Condominiums International; industry publisher Carl Burlingame; statistician Dr. Richard L. Ragatz; from ALDA, Gary Terry and Gary Burnett; and for research and editing, John Murray, Marge Lennon, Dick Dennis and Susan Leisner.

For the use of photographs of its interval units abroad, I am indebted to Interval International.